TRUE TALES OF TERROR

AND THE CAT CAME BACK

TRUE TALES OF ANIMAL SPIRIT HAUNTINGS

TRUE TALES OF TERROR

AND THE CAT CAME BACK

TRUE TALES OF ANIMAL SPIRIT HAUNTINGS

JOSHUA WARREN

ROSEN
PUBLISHING

New York

This edition published in 2016 by:
The Rosen Publishing Group, Inc.
29 East 21st Street
New York, NY 10010

Library of Congress Cataloging-in-Publication Date

Warren, Joshua P.
And the cat came back: true tales of animal spirit hauntings/Joshua P. Warren.
    pages cm.—(True tales of terror)
Includes bibliographical references and index.
ISBN 978-1-4994-6156-5 (library bound)
1. Animal ghosts. 2. Extrasensory perception in animals. I. Title.
BF1484.W369 2015
133.1'4—dc23

                                                        2015001118

Manufactured in the United States of America

First published as *Pet Ghosts: Animal Encounters from Beyond the Grave* by New Page Books/Career Press, copyright © 2006, Joshua P. Warren.

DEDICATION

**To Lauren,
With Love**

Acknowledgments

The breadth of received information necessary to write a book is almost too great for expressed gratitude. In stating my appreciation for the bulk of material, I always fear leaving out a valuable contributor. Therefore, I must generally thank everyone who was kind enough to volunteer experiences and insight. But I must thank a few particular folks who went above and beyond to help me with this project.

Nick Redfern, a busy and successful author, was so generous and altruistic that it's easy to understand his own success. Lynn Jackson was so kind and thorough in sharing her database of photos and experiences that I predict her research will make a significant impact on this field. The legend of Brad Steiger accurately reflects his true warmth, kindness, and sage-like wisdom. And Loren Coleman is the most meticulous, dedicated researcher in his field, always open to helping me.

Sometimes, the simplest phrases are the best. Thank you.

CONTENTS

Introduction

   As a professional paranormal investigator, I was especially interested in the death of my dog, a miniature daschund named Nellie, in 2002. When she apparently came back from the other side, my house functioned as a laboratory for measuring her ghost. It started with strange noises at night—the familiar sound of her whimpers and barks in the empty rooms. It would take a second for me to realize, to remind myself, that she was dead. Was my mind playing tricks on me? Was I hearing something else, perhaps squeaks in the wall structure that my mind interpreted as dog sounds because I was so used to hearing them? And then, fleeting by sometimes, her tiny toenails scampered on the wooden floor. Was Nellie back? Or was some aspect of her still resonating in the environment like a recording? Or was it something else altogether?

   I took out my barrage of gear: electromagnetic field meters, electrostatic field detectors, IR cameras, and so on. These are tools that allow us to tap into an invisible realm. For example, think about radio waves. You can't see them, feel them, hear them, smell them, or taste them, but if you have a simple little tool (a radio, tuned to their frequency) you can tap into a wealth of intelligent information. This kind of information exists around us in a nearly infinite range of energies. I studied the physical environment for some objective proof of Nellie's ghost. What I discovered sent me on a journey of exploration. When thinking of ghosts, we usually envision people, but what about animals? Are they any different than us? This book will show you what I found.

1 A History of Spectral Animals

Because this is a book about ghosts, I must first clarify how a *ghost* is defined. Actually, we must deal with two phenomena: *ghost* animals and *ghostly* animals. Later we'll explore the physical aspects of these elements, but for now, specific terminology and definition is necessary for efficient understanding. These definitions are not based on current scientific proof, but on reports, and the documentation of spectral creatures for thousands of years. If such recordings are sometimes accurate, and we will assume they are, *ghost* animals and *ghostly* animals can also each be divided into two subcategories.

A *ghost animal* is some paranormal aspect of the physical form and/or mental presence that appears to exist apart from the original, physical form. Therefore, to be considered a ghost, it is essential for a creature to have occupied the physical realm (the same plane our present human bodies occupy), at some point. The two subcategories are *entities* and *imprints*.

An *entity ghost animal* is an interactive, unpredictable, aware apparition that appears to be a spirit and remains conscious apart from, usually after the death of, an animal. This is the sort of phantom most think of when visualizing a ghost. An example would be a pet that seems to come back after death and nudge you on the leg, in unpredictable ways, to gain your attention.

An *imprint ghost animal* is non-interactive, redundant, and appears to have no immediate awareness of its environment. An example would be horses drawing a ghostly stagecoach along a regular path. Perhaps the procession heralds a corpse, and both the inanimate coach and the horses appear as visions, like a movie being replayed, looped in one area. Observing them may depend on mysterious environmental conditions or the physiological/technical aspects of the observer.

Next we have the second main category: *ghostly animals.* They differ from the previous category in that they do not necessarily have to be apparitions that appear apart from the occupation of a physical form. We can loosely define them as creatures that exhibit, or facilitate, properties inexplicable to known physical laws. The two subcategories are *elementals* and *harbingers.*

An *elemental ghostly animal* is one that may have never occupied a physical body. Take for example the hellhounds, also known as black dogs, of the United Kingdom. They are perceived as demonic, ominous creatures from some netherworld. Often elementals resemble regular animals in the physical realm, but look a little different. Hellhounds are frequently described as having red, glowing eyes and are much larger than known living dogs. Such slight variations in their appearance are common earmarks of an elemental beast.

Harbinger ghostly animals may indeed be physical animals in our realm, but they carry with them spiritual energy. Such creatures might have been specifically charged with paranormal energy, such as a witch's *familiar*—a minion or messenger of a magician's spell. Or it's possible that some creatures are simply attracted to concentrated pools of energy, either good or bad, due to a sensitivity we don't yet understand. That animal's presence can also indicate the presence of the energy, but whether or not the creature brought the energy, or somehow caused it to exist, is indeterminate.

I had the misfortune of personally encountering what I think were most likely harbingers. A few years ago, due to a personal and professional falling out with an old friend, I felt he intentionally placed a curse on me. This man often practiced magic, and even introduced me to the reality of the subject. It therefore came as no great surprise when I was struck by a long, rapid string of bad luck. One after the other, I suffered mechanical failures (cars and a well pump "dying"), electronic mishaps (computers and similar devices frying), financial difficulties, and finally problems with personal relationships. Without delving deeply into magic, I should explain that thoughts are as solid and physical as bullets. Otherwise, how could your thoughts control the movement of your body? When persistently and ceremoniously concentrated over time, thoughts cause a tangible impact on the thinker's target. This black magician was apparently focusing some very nasty things in my direction. It all came to a head when the harbingers arrived.

Living in the rural Blue Ridge Mountains and having stayed up late, I napped in bed on a lazy Sunday afternoon. My girlfriend, Lauren, rested beside me on the bed watching television. She listened to the tube via headphones so I would not be disturbed; she laid on the side of the bed facing the room's only doorway, with me on the opposite side. At one point during my shallow slumber, I heard strange sounds, like crisp plastic being crinkled, finally so distinct that I awoke and tugged on Lauren's sleeve. She slipped down the headphones and I asked her if she'd heard that weird noise. Lauren, rather nonchalantly, said she may have heard some slight noise of no consequence, replaced the headset, and returned her attention to the television. Half-asleep, and satisfied with her response, I rolled back over to continue napping. At that point, something extraordinary occurred. A voice spoke to me: *There is a snake over there*; it was quite unfamiliar and androgynous. I opened my heavy eyelids, leaned toward the side of the mattress and was horrified to find a thick, black snake, easily 6 feet in length, only inches from my face. His cold eyes stared directly into mine, body length pausing in midslither, heading straight toward me. Instantly, I sprang forth cursing, amazed and dizzied by the sight. The sound of crinkling plastic was from his length passing over some thin plastic bags on our floor.

For the next 10 minutes I wrestled with the snake. At the moment our eyes locked, an epic struggle became clear to us both. The serpent hissed and struck repeatedly, the musky stench of his reptilian fear oozing in the air. Though such black snakes are not venomous, I understand their mouths are full of rotting bacteria and their strong teeth so curved and sharp that, once lodged deeply in flesh, the creature often cannot pull its own diseased mouth from the prey. Trying to escape, he'd shoot under furniture and I'd grab his tail, whipping him back out, his muscular, arched form striking toward me again, scales shining. Eventually, thanks to the help of a long, gripping, mechanical device (intended to remove objects from high shelves) I got a hold on his neck and dumped the snake in a trashcan. Hurriedly, trembling with adrenaline, I rushed the aggressive serpent outside and disposed of him with a machete.

Upon my return to the house, Lauren and I were a nervous wreck, especially because I woke up to this drama. I went to the bathroom, on the opposite end of the house, to wash the snake's stench from my hands. Then I heard Lauren shriek. "Oh my God, there's another one!" Popping my head out of the bathroom, I couldn't believe my eyes.

As a child, I remember weathered, old-time mountaineers speaking of snakes with seasoned hatred: *When you kill one, another will come along to avenge it.* Typically, this concept is rejected by scientists. But, sure enough, less than 10 minutes after the initial episode, a second black snake was slithering in from the opposite end of the house. To this day, I'm not sure how they gained access. For me, it was back to square one.

The same kind of struggle ensued, and it ended with the same result. I finally got the second snake outside and killed it as well. I know some of you will fault me as an ignorant brute for killing these snakes and against that charge I have no strong defense, other than ensuring these particular serpents would never slither into my domain again. At the time, that was my only concern. Having personally handled and killed them, I assure you they were physical creatures. Yet, once the initial shock of the event wore off, I was struck by many extraordinary qualities of the encounter.

First, for days afterward I assumed it was Lauren's voice that told me a snake was slithering toward me. Though it did not sound like her, she was the only other person there—presuming the warning issued from her lips was only natural. However, upon hearing me recount the experience to others, my girlfriend was surprised by my perception and strongly clarified that she had *not* given any such warning; in fact, she didn't know the first serpent was present until I sprang at its sight. So whose voice gave the warning? I do not know. Some might suggest an angel whispered in my ear, alerting me to the impending threat. Of course, that raises an even greater question. What is an angel? As a person who does not accept reality on mere faith, I cannot say. But there was some protective force vocalizing the situation, at least to my perception. I heard it as a sound, but could I have heard it even without ears? Maybe it was my own subconscious, more acute in my mental state on the boundary of sleep and full consciousness.

Why were there two snakes? Why did the first one, perhaps having traveled through the entire house (if it entered on the same end as the second serpent), slither right past Lauren's side of the bed and go straight for me? And to compound the complexity of the situation, in discussions reflecting on the event it was revealed that the physical position of the second snake, in terms of its body's orientation to the room, appeared different to each Lauren and me. She recalls the creature at a somewhat different place and angle, feet away from my recollection. Is this merely the product of two people, in a state of panic, perceiving the same threat from different mindsets? Or is there something of a more dark and sinister nature at work here—perhaps something that calls into question the nature of reality itself? There's no doubt about it: the snakes were real;

the head of one is presently preserved in an alcohol-filled jar in my basement. But the experience, and the context, seemed surreal. I accepted them as ultimate harbingers of the black magic being directed toward me, and quickly took action to finally combat these nefarious forces.

After utilizing some ceremonious exercises to deflect the curse back to its source, things quickly improved in my life. It was a valuable learning experience overall. In this strange case, you can more clearly see how complicated the subject of *phantimals* (paranormal creatures that appear more animal-like than human-like) can be. We are not only talking about the mere spirit of a deceased creature returning from the other side, but also that mysterious relationship between some animals and paranormal energy fields. Are they indeed the messengers or simply attracted, like flies that can travel miles, appearing on a corpse with uncanny speed, only minutes after the time of death? Fortunately ghosts of the snakes never plagued me, perhaps in part due to my "mental cleansing" of the situation. But some of the oldest references to phantimals feature serpents quite prominently.

Ancient Times

One of the oldest, and certainly paranormal, documents is the Bible. Only a couple pages into the book (Genesis 3), a serpent, acting as the instrument of Satan, is portrayed as completely altering the fate of mankind, diabolically tempting Eve to eat forbidden fruit against God's wishes. Eve's submission is considered the first sin and dooms all humans thereafter to a life of hardship, apart from the paradise of Eden originally intended for faithful servants. The story implies that snakes once may have had legs, or even wings, because God penalizes the creature by proclaiming "Because thou hast done this, thou art cursed above all cattle, and above every beast of the field; upon thy belly shalt thou go, and dust shalt thou eat all the days of thy life."

This is a very bizarre account, as it also implies the serpent somehow willingly participated in the process of conducting the devil's wishes, hence its punishment. It is unclear if the particular snake was in physical form the entire time, or able to switch to an intangible messenger when possessed, and then back to physical when Satan left. As you will continue to see, this is a perplexing aspect of many phantimals. There are also the problems of determining whether or not a creature is physical based solely on limited human observation (we'll especially explore this later when addressing *cryptids*) and understanding the nature of physicality itself. Everything is simply energy, and we only consider physical those energies resonating at a frequency and wavelength that will resist our own, occupying the same realm of resonance as our human bodies.

Snakes are used again early in the Bible for an important role that potentially contradicts the symbology of Eve's encounter. In Exodus 7, Moses confronts the tyrannical Pharaoh, demanding freedom for the Israelites. To demonstrate his divine power, God instructs Moses to toss his staff on the floor before the Pharaoh, transforming it into a serpent. Moses does so, and the royal sorcerers duplicate the feat with their rods. However, Moses's snake then devours theirs, and the creature turns back into a staff. As the story proceeds, the staff is used as the symbol of God's power because Moses is told to incorporate the instrument when triggering miraculous events, such as turning all Egypt's water into blood. In this case, the serpent is apparently worthy to represent God's will and, through its relationship to the staff, a conduit of para-normal energy. For better or worse, snakes therefore symbolize an overwhelming connection to extreme power, transformation, and the ability to blur the line between concepts of good and evil. Incidentally, in the Exodus story, swarms of animals like frogs, flies, and locusts are also used to plague Egypt for God's will. Such "lower" life-forms are seen as easy to manipulate by higher levels of consciousness.

These situations with Eve and Moses may be some of the earliest scenarios differentiating an *animal* from a pet. If you think carefully about what separates animals (domesticated or otherwise) from pets, you will see there are many variables to be considered. At what point does an animal become a pet? After perusing a number of dictionary definitions intended for general discussions of the terms, I have constructed this loose definition of a *pet* for our purposes: a specific animal that apparently shares a mutually beneficial relationship with a specific entity, or entities, usually augmented by a higher degree of control by the involved entity or entities. Note that this definition does not require, in any way, a finite measure of control, care, or emotional attachment, as is often the case in such relevant definitions. Though we usually think of pets in relation to humans, according to this principle, we can make a case for the Genesis serpent being a pet of Satan, and the Exodus serpent a pet of God.

Regardless of the creature's presence in this physical realm, or some intangible dimension, in Genesis the serpent is cooperating with an entity: Lucifer. In the Exodus story, the serpent is cooperating with God, however limited its existence in our plane. In both cases we see elements, consistent with our definition of a pet, that confirm these animals as being special as opposed to the broad population of wild specimens. Therefore, to be completely accurate, you must first appreciate the various kinds of phantimals, then understand the difference between those that do and do not qualify as pets. Otherwise, it is impossible to express the vast, beautiful range of phantimals, and their meanings, and be faithful to your expectations from this work.

Scholars believe that *The Epic of Gilgamesh* is even older than the Bible. This sweeping adventure is Babylonian, based on earlier Sumerian legends, and may have been written around 2100 BCE. Not only does it include a prominent ghostly encounter, but the entity is that of Enkidu, a hairy, man-like creature similar to our modern concept of the sasquatch. Though cryptids will be thoroughly addressed later in the book, we can consider Enkidu an animal because he was not identified as a true human. Yet this beast could speak, and we can think of him as a phantimal at the very least upon his return from the dead to visit with his old friend, the great king Gilgamesh. This passage exemplifies the encounter:

> *Enkidu's shadow rose slowly toward the living*
> *and the brothers, tearful and weak,*
> *tried to hug, tried to speak,*
> *tried and failed to do anything but sob.*
> *"Speak to me please, dear brother," whispered*
>   *Gilgamesh.*
> *"Tell me of death and where you are."*
> *"Not willingly do I speak of death,"*

said Enkidu in slow reply.
"But if you wish to sit for a brief
time, I will describe where I do stay."
"Yes," his brother said in early grief.
"All my skin and all my bones are dead now.
All my skin and all my bones are now dead.
"Oh no" cried Gilgamesh without relief.
"Oh no," sobbed one enclosed by grief.

The ancient culture applying the most extensive spirituality to animals may have been the Egyptians. They believed a variety of gods and goddesses occupied particular species, or species hybrids. For example, dog-headed baboons represented Thoth, the god of writing, and Khonsu, the moon god. Crocodiles exemplified Ammut, who punished evildoers. A sacred animal especially associated with the afterlife was the cat. Whether wild or domesticated, they were called *miu* or *mii*, which means *he or she that mews*. Thousands of cats were mummified to facilitate their existence in an afterlife. In fact, the creature was held so sacred that, according to scientists at the Natural History Museum in London, X-rays reveal that many cat mummies had their necks intentionally snapped to expedite journeys to the other side—an unfortunate irony for a beast considered sacred!

Though literature from North Africa is some of the most popular and well-recorded, less specific tales originate from most parts of the world. Chinese astrology is famous for its association between animals and spiritual characteristics. Creatures like dogs, rats, goats, and monkeys are used to exemplify personality traits. The one unfamiliar, some would say mythical, animal to which such traits are ascribed is the dragon. Does this give the dragon more credibility, being that it was grouped with animals we know to be real? Dragons, respected in Asian culture for thousands of years, can clearly be called phantimals. They are serpentine beasts that can fly and breathe fire, often considered auspicious. Though most prominent in Asian cultures, even the Bible mentions the fire-breathing dragon Leviathan in Job 41:

> *Out of his mouth go burning lamps, and sparks of fire leap out. Out of his nostrils goeth smoke, as out of a seething pot or caldron. His breath kindleth coals, and a flame goeth out of his mouth...He maketh the deep to boil like a pot: he maketh the sea like a pot of ointment.*

In modern times, we know of no animal that can breathe fire. Surely if a creature of this sort once roamed the Earth, it crossed the boundary between our concept of physical and non-physical. Our current scientists cannot explain how a beast might produce fire given our understanding of physical biology.

Ancient Americans strongly based their culture on an appreciation for animals' mystical traits. Some Native Americans still see animals as windows to the Great Spirit, each type offering different views. This is exemplified by the Totem poles that certain peoples from the Pacific Northwest make. *Totems* are the spirits that manifest through animals, such as power through the bear and planning via the squirrel. Various aspects of life are facilitated by these invisible forces and delivered through nature.

Perhaps one of the most chilling apparitions in ancient American culture has been the wendigo. This beast blurs the line between humans and creatures. *Wendigos* are hairy giants that were once normal, living humans. However, these people "died," at very least in a spiritual sense, after resorting to cannibalism. Such a horrible practice transformed them into deformed, bloodthirsty animals, similar to the European concept of humans becoming vampires. And, just as a vampire can shapeshift into other creatures, such as bats, wolves, or owls, wendigos can also shapeshift, even back to their original human forms. But when seen in true form, these shaggy monsters have glowing eyes, long yellow fangs, and extended, dripping tongues. This spectral animal's relationship to humans places it in a special category, as is so often the case in these ancient tales.

It's noteworthy that even in modern time belief in wendigos has been so strong as to inspire serial murders. Jack Fiddler, a Canadian Cree Indian, claimed to have killed at least 14 "wendigos" in his life, and was tried in 1907 for the murder of a woman in his tribe. He and his son said she was in fact a wendigo, but Fiddler was imprisoned for murder at the age of 87. Such instances reinforce the connection between ancient culture and present ideas regarding humans and animals.

Australian Aborigines revered animal spirits as much as other ancient cultures, applying mystical meaning to creatures, especially those visiting in dreams. The Yowie was a mysterious, hairy, animal-like spirit that represented death. Its specific origin is unknown, but in Tasmania, a more familiar type of phantimal has been reported near the Richmond Bridge. There, a hulking black dog haunts. He appears at night when potentially vulnerable people, like petite women or small children, intend to cross and escorts them over safely. Afterward, the helpful canine meanders off, dissolving into the evening air. These black dogs are especially prominent in Europe and are well-recorded in the Middle Ages and Victorian era.

From the Middle Ages
Through Victorian Times

Understandably, in ancient lore specific kinds of animals are not always clearly identified. Information was scattered and inconsistent, and our current accounts are vague remnants of what has been translated many times and pieced together by a long line of historians. But due to the German invention of the Gutenberg printing press in 1456, European ghost stories from the Middle Ages through Victorian times are some of the best-documented early accounts clarifying particular creatures.

As in the ancient Egyptian civilization, cats played a prominent role in shades of this era. The idea of cats being associated with spiritual evil was greatly enhanced by the publication of the *Malleus Maleficarum* (*The Hammer of Witches*) in 1487. Authors Heinrich Kramer and James Sprenger were Dominican Catholic friars who helped spearhead the witch-hunting craze of the 15th through 17th centuries. During its time, sales of the book were only exceeded by the Bible (which says "Thou shalt not suffer a witch to live," in Exodus 22:18), and up to millions of people may have been tortured and killed due to its influence as a handbook during the Inquisition. Cats were directly described as possible tools of the devil:

> *...a workman was one day chopping some wood to burn in his house. A large cat suddenly appeared and began to attack him, and when he was driving it off, another even larger one came and attacked him*

with the first more fiercely. And when he again tried to drive them away, behold, three of them together attacked him, jumping up at his face, and biting and scratching his legs. In great fright and, as he said, more panic-stricken than he had ever been, he crossed himself and, leaving his work, fell upon the cats, which were swarming over the wood and again leaping at his face and throat, and with difficulty drove them away by beating one on the head, another on the legs, and another on the back.

Soon after the incident, the workman is suddenly arrested by town magistrates and thrown into a dungeon without explanation. Days later, a judge accuses him of beating three respected women of the town, each of them "bewailing their blows." The astonished man replies "I remember that I struck some creatures at that time, but they were not women." The book goes on to say:

Now concerning this it may be asked, whether the devils appeared thus in assumed shapes without the presence of the witches, or whether the witches were actually present, converted by some glamour into the shapes of those beasts. And in answering this it should be said that, although it was equally possible for the devils to act in either way, it is rather presumed that it was done in the second manner. For when the devils attacked the workman in the shapes of cats, they could suddenly, by local motion through the air, transfer the women to their houses with the blows which they received as cats from the workman; and no one doubts that this was because of a mutual pact formerly made between them...They used the phantasm of a cat, an animal which is, in the Scriptures, an appropriate symbol of the perfidious, just as a dog is the symbol of preachers; for cats are always setting snares for each other. And the Order of Preaching Friars was represented in its first Founder by a dog barking against heresy.

In calling cats *perfidious* (tending to betray) vehicles for witches, this popular guide immortalized a connection between felines and the supernatural for better or for worse. Conversely, dogs are seen as representing the holy viewpoint, thereby elevating the classic perception of dogs and cats as eternal foes. Clearly, the idea that witches can transform into felines made a huge impact on the European culture, evident to this day as traditional sorcerers are seldom seen without a purring sidekick and black cats, long thought to harbor bad luck, are popular targets for Halloween tricks. It's no wonder that cats and dogs are not only our favorite pets, but also associated with ghostly activity. Of the two, dogs are most often mentioned as apparitions from this period.

Photo courtesy of Nick Redfern.
The area surrounding the church at England's Widecombe-in-the-Moor has been haunted by creatures similar to black dogs for centuries. On October 21, 1638, the church also suffered an extraordinary lightening storm, killing four people and injuring 62.

To this day, the most famous canine apparitions in Europe are those of the United Kingdom, especially the "black dogs;" a general term for shadowy canine-like creatures often accompanying doom. The concept was especially popularized in the Sherlock Holmes mystery, *The Hound of the Baskervilles*, written by Sir Arthur Conan Doyle, an author who publicly upheld a lifelong interest in the paranormal. These creatures can fulfill a wide variety of purposes, from revenge to protection to omens. In his 1913 book *Animal Ghosts*, Elliott O'Donnell makes the following important statement: "As to what class of spirits the spectre dog belongs, that is impossible to say. At the most we can only surmise, and I should think the chances of its being the actual phantasm of some dead dog or an elemental are about equal." In other words, we can't say for certain whether these phantimals are the products of once-living canines, or originating from another realm altogether. Personally, I suspect they are indeed elementals because they are often larger than usual dogs and exhibit behavior apparently driven by purposes transcending the mere survival instincts of a normal animal from our realm.

Some particular examples are the *faery dogs* from the Highlands of Scotland. These large dogs, with short tails and long feet, are actually a mossy green in color, despite the popular moniker of "black dogs." They appear to be guarding a cavern of some sort on the Isle of Tiree, and bark three times before viciously attacking. Therefore, obviously, no one living can say what happens past the third bark. The idea of these beings as foreboding guards is a common theme, also exhibited by the *galleytrot*.

Galleytrots are tall, eerie specters that appear as hounds walking upright, sometimes with body parts seeming human-like. They are most often seen around ancient European burial grounds or sites of hidden treasure. As is usual with such beings, a sighting is considered a freakish omen of death, so observers usually flee in terror. We therefore have little information about such beings, but they are sometimes dressed in human clothes, may even be capable of speaking, and are certainly different than any ordinary creature on the physical planet.

Of course, the most chilling of black dogs, and perhaps the most well-known, are the hellhounds or devil dogs. These massive black canines, with searing eyes of fire, have been considered members of Satan's hunting pack. They are always associated with negative events. In many cases, it's not even important to actually view the beasts. Simply hearing their blood-curdling howls break a midnight's stillness is enough to appreciate their impact. According to legend, such beasts not only guard the Devil's most sacred secrets, but aggress toward any party Lucifer targets for spiritual attack. In some cases, the packs are even headless, and the most outstanding have frequently been sighted near Cornwall, England.

Though the earliest report of a black dog probably came from France in 856 CE—a creature that briefly appeared during an evening church service, eyes glowing, when the room's torches suddenly extinguished—the most outstanding early experiences were in England, in August of 1577. Strangely enough these encounters also occurred during church services. The creature in France harmlessly appeared and disappeared, and we have no clear understanding of its implications, but the animal that interrupted a stormy Sunday morning service in Bungay, England, was certainly a hellhound.

To this day, a black dog crests the Bungay coat of arms

Without explanation, the beast, physically described as a typical giant, raven dog with blazing eyes, appeared in an aisle of St. Mary's Church and violently sprung on a member of the congregation. By the time the hysterical patrons realized what was happening, at least three members of the church were dead, some with throats and limbs torn away, some crushed by fallen masonry due to the leaping beast's weight, and others scorched and shriveled by the phantom's energy. The region's storm churned with, according to Abraham Fleming's pamphlet of the day, "darkness, rain, hail, thunder, and lightning as was never seen the like." Shortly thereafter, a black dog, perhaps the same one, interrupted another church service at Blythburgh Church in Suffolk, only around 10 miles (16 km) away. Mauling and murder continued there. Once its bloodthirsty work was done, the powerful hound galloped out a door, leaving deep, black burn marks on the surrounding wood. An old verse records the Bungay event:

> All down the church in midst of
> Fire, the hellish monster flew
> And, passing onward to the quire,
> He many people slew.

These kinds of stories are particularly interesting. The incident at Bungay made such a realistic impact that the hellhound was incorporated into the town's coat of arms, and to this day the supposed burn marks can be seen at Blythburg.

The dog's purported ability to savagely kill, and its having a weight heavy enough to destroy parts of the Bungay building, undeniably implies its solid existence in our physical realm. However, the fact it severely burned humans, and the wooden doorway, plus the sheer scope and magnitude of its chaotic destruction and mysterious origin, are not consistent with any known normal animal. This curious combination of, dare we say, natural and *supernatural* qualities makes it extremely difficult to understand such a being. Regardless of whether or not such beasts spend most of the time in some other realm, non-physical to us, when they *do* assume a presence in our realm, they are absolutely tangible and even augmented by physical powers misunderstood by present scientific views. They are certainly phantimals, and yet phantimals are not exclusively nonphysical. On the contrary, they seem to shift between the frequencies of our physical dimension and others, fully interactive participant in whatever realm they occupy at any given time.

Though European ghost dogs are the best-documented, such creatures have been seen around the world. South Africans have long told of the *wolhaarhond*, which is considered an omen of doom and is generally described as a shaggy beast usually seen from a distance, only fully recognizable if the unfortunate observer gets within feet of the apparition. As opposed to classic black dogs that may only have glowing eyes, the wolhaarhond's entire body is surrounded by devilish crimson light. Such an appearance is more typical of traditional apparitions materializing in luminous, almost electrically enhanced, forms.

Though it is never surprising that dogs and cats should be recognized in spectral literature, given their long histories as pets, modern humans may be surprised by how horses are prominently mentioned in that context, as well. After all, the presence of a horse is a novelty for most in our era of automobiles and airplanes. But in days past, even a person with no desire or need for a dog or cat often relied on a relationship with horses for transportation. It is therefore not surprising that horse apparitions may be the most widely documented of all. Of course, we must wonder whether this is due to an increased presence of equine spirits or the simple fact that such large creatures are easier to observe. This is a question that frequently crops up in the discussion of animal phantoms. Given the fleeing nature of so many creatures, how can we be sure of whether or not an animal briefly observed is actually a normal, physical specimen or a ghost? Quite simply, we cannot.

Horse apparitions are frequently seen with ghostly human counterparts. The best examples may be the headless horsemen. Tales of galloping, pitch-black steeds mounted by furious, decapitated riders have lingered for hundreds of years, especially found in some of the earliest German and Scandinavian legends, as documented in the 1700s by folklorist Karl Musaus. Such specters are usually the product of wars. A revered officer, set on battle, who suddenly loses his head, exists in a state of delirious confusion. Energy of the tortured man, frustrated by his inability to complete the fight, especially with adrenaline pumping, may burn a hole between this dimension and the next. Headless horsemen are unable to tell the difference between friend and foe, and so attack anyone unfortunate enough to cross their paths. The strangest part is the very fact that they ride horses. If a soldier is beheaded, but the animal survives, why should the creature be doomed to appear as a misty slave of his master? If the horse is killed at the same time, then it makes sense. Otherwise, we must wonder if the beheaded chooses from some stable of phantasmal equines in the netherworld or if the soldier's horse instantly transforms from a physical to nonphysical beast by means of a process misunderstood by science. On the other hand, in some cases they might simply be imprints, therefore negating the necessity for the horse death. Regardless of the origin, these creatures carrying tormented human souls are certainly impressive phantimals.

Headless horsemen of the United States were popularized by Washington Irving's 1819 fictional short story , "The Legend of Sleepy Hollow," and the 1869 publication of *The Headless Horseman* by Captain Mayne Reid. Unlike Irving's tale, Captain Reid's book is based on true accounts from Texas, personally investigated by the author. Among Native Americans, wraiths astride horses were not an uncommon sight, even if the riders were not beheaded. Perhaps the most dramatic example comes from Chimney Rock, North Carolina.

Chimney Rock is lush with Cherokee Indian legends. The most outstanding is a terrible battle that sometimes rages in the sky at sunset. The horizon turns to wispy, bluish fog, and from the seething clouds emerge two armies, with hundreds of horses, engaging head-on in a desperate clash. This epic struggle was observed by whites as early as 1811. Being tiny figures on the ground, pioneers would gawk up at the churning purplish scene playing out in the heavens on a vast, awesome scale. Though there is no historical basis for this original event, those who witness the rare display are most impressed by the snorts and cries of the distressed horses surrounded by rampant death and murder.

Another well-known ghost horse and non-headless rider duo is Herne the Hunter in England's Windsor Forest. Apparently, around the year 1400, a rugged man named Herne was a forest keeper for King Richard II. He spent most of his time alone in the woods, concealed, looking out for poachers and trespassers, with whom he dealt harshly. With time, due to gradual loss of his youth and outdoors skill, or fear of being disgraced by some perverse offense, he hanged himself from an oak tree. Since then, the mighty hunter's charging apparition, high astride a black steed, has terrified hundreds of trespassers. The protective Herne is said to wear a stag's skull on his head, its long, twisting horns making the whole display beastly and surreal. In 1843, author W. Harrison Ainsworth described the sight in his novel Windsor Castle:

> *...a wild, spectral object, possessing a slight resemblance to a human being, clad in the skin of a deer and wearing on its head a sort of helmet, formed of the skull of a stag, from which branched a large pair of antlers. It was surrounded by a blue phosphoric light.*

But this chilling apparition was even recorded much earlier, in 1599, by none other than William Shakespeare in *The Merry Wives of Windsor*:

> *There is an old tale goes that Herne the Hunter,*
> *Sometime a keeper here in Windsor Forrest,*
> *Doth all the winter-time, at still midnight,*
> *Walk round about an oak, with great ragg'd horns;*

And there he blasts the tree and takes the cattle
And makes milch-kine yield blood and shakes a chain
In a most hideous and dreadful manner:
You have heard of such a spirit, and well you know
The superstitious idle-headed eld
Received and did deliver to our age
This tale of Herne the hunter for a truth.

It's easy to imagine horses on land being utilized by humans, whether in this life or the next. But, amazingly, not all horse-like shades are restricted to the dry earth. This is best exemplified by the Scottish *kelpie*. These creatures are often called "water devils," and are basically deceptive aquatic spirits that manifest as young, healthy horses grazing near waterways. When someone inevitably tries to climb on its back, the creature bolts for water, splashes like thunderclaps, intentionally drowning the human. At that point, the horse may transform into a more evil humanoid form, having successfully lured a person to doom. No one knows why kelpies hate humans, though they've been seen for hundreds of years, even described by author Stewart W. Grant in 1823's *Popular Superstitions of the Highlanders of Scotland.* Some Scots believe that if a man is strong enough to strap a bridle on a kelpie, the creature will submit and be a valuable resource the rest of its life. However, if the bridle is ever removed, or somehow slips away, the escaping kelpie will place a horrible curse on the man who restrained it.

Though cats, dogs, and horses have been popular phantimals in history, it is, of course, impossible to completely address the wide variety of animals documented. Virtually every kind of creature has made a spectral appearance in some culture. When it comes to variety of species, I must at least mention the *kirk-grim*. For hundreds of years, especially in Europe and the Americas, it has been customary to kill and bury an animal (or simply bury one alive) at the site of a newly constructed church or graveyard. The spirit of the sacrificed creature is intended to guard the property against vandals and others with disrespectful intentions. In some instances, even humans were murdered for the task; in that case the resultant wraith was called an *ankou*. An important estate may require multiple animals to be sacrificed, and some of the most prominent were lambs, pigs, cows, goats, and chickens. In 1893, author T. Thistleton Dyer wrote about these phantoms in *Ghost World*. He specifically commented on lambs in churches, saying they often resided in the building's tower. If a lamb is seen leaping about the grounds when service is not in session, it is an omen that a parishioner's child will soon die.

Perhaps the most difficult phantimals to put in perspective are those with wings. An owl may be a witch's familiar, vampires have their bats, and ancient Greeks and Egyptians revered the phoenix, a bird (probably eagle or peacock) that would die every few years in an inferno then rise, alive, from the ashes. It's virtually impossible to draw conclusions about winged organisms because they are so fleeting and transient. The remote exception is birds that appear by their own will at, or near, the time of someone's death, such as crows, ravens, swans, owls, or robins (in particular if the same animal perpetually visits the same family). It's generally easy to see such winged creatures and draw subjective conclusions, but difficult to study them from some stable, controlled perspective: such is definitely the case with insects. How would you know if an insect at which you've been swatting is a ghost? In fact, annoying insects *do* frequently vanish all of a sudden. Might these be specters? There is really no reliable research into this subject. Nonetheless, take a look at the European spunkies.

Spunkies are ghosts that supposedly materialize as small, white moths. Best known in Scotland, they are the spirits of unbaptized children who met with untimely deaths. These lost entities wander aimlessly until Judgment Day, sometimes filling the innocent role of helping newly-deceased human spirits transition and sometimes leading ships off course to disaster. Vessel lights shining on a cloud of spunkies can reflect and appear like a beacon light. Such a confusing sight makes some ships steer into craggy, treacherous rocks, but whether or not this is inadvertent or the spunkies intend to harbinger such doom is unknown. Clearly, the idea of exploring subtle insect ghosts presses into the extreme fringe of paranormal research.

When addressing these phantimals from the past, we are greatly limited by mankind's infantile understanding of ghostly activity, not to mention difficulty in clarifying exactly what was observed. Even now, with our superior technology, the nature of phantoms is deeply mysterious. Nonetheless, phantimals are experienced now as much as ever. The history of reports is a valuable foundation, proving the longevity of these human observations; but now let's bring these experiences up to date. In the coming text we'll explore basic scientific concepts of how it may be possible for these ghosts to exist. And then we'll examine accounts that don't lie in dusty old books, but come straight from the mouths of living men and women whom I've interviewed, open to question for more details. It may be difficult to discriminate between a normal and paranormal animal cavorting in the wild. Seeing a pet, however, is a whole different story. The intimate contact between a pet and its owner, including the owner's ability to identify his or her specific pet as opposed to other examples of the species, is an important scientific tool. Details of modern pet ghosts can broaden our understanding of how the universe works, and how humans fit into the picture along with animals. But first we should analyze what a pet ghost may actually be, and how it can survive physical death.

2 What Is an Animal Ghost?

I'm suddenly struck by the words of an ignorant man. Currently, I host a radio show about strange and paranormal activity, and through the years I've probably been interviewed in every English-speaking country of the world. Radio work, particularly when done live, is a valuable tool for research. It provides the opportunity for instant interaction with a wide range of people and their views, and generally offers more unedited time for discussion than television shows do. Recently I was the guest on a "general-subject" afternoon program, in the Southeastern United States, and a man named Jim called in quite upset with me.

I'd been talking about animal ghosts, and this discussion triggered the caller's wrath. He was a self-proclaimed die-hard Christian, and spat that he was offended that I had suggested an animal might have a spirit. In his opinion, and by his interpretation of the Bible, man was clearly separated from beasts. He stressed that we are superior to them in all ways, that they exist as soulless meat robots, and that it was disgraceful to imply that humans and animals could be equal, in any way, on a spiritual level.

My immediate reply was that, to begin with, it's ignorant to assume that ghosts are dependent on the existence of a soul or spirit at all. Considering apparitions of cars, ships, and building structures have been reported, the experience of seeing a specter may have much more to do with catching a glimpse of the past—the ol' imprint phenomenon. But aside from that, let's address the possibility of an animal having a soul just like a human. Of course, the first real issue is how we define a soul. In my opinion, we can call a soul some aspect of a being that is able to retain consciousness, personality, memories, and interactivity apart from having a physical body. Jim seemed to share that definition, and was adamant that animals turn directly to dust upon death and every part of them is gone forever; and if that were not the case, then we'd be run over by billions of animal ghosts from all of history right?

We cannot scientifically prove that a soul exists, not to mention it having the ability to survive physical death. Being open-minded, we must accept the possibility that, regardless of personal, subjective experiences with apparent entities, a soul *may not* exist. On the broad scale necessary for scientific proof, we can't definitely rule out hallucinations, that is to say an experience that only occurs inside a person's head, generated by that person's imagination. But if a spirit (and I use "spirit" and "soul" interchangeably) does exist within living creatures, I see no good reason to separate humans from any other organisms, no matter how great or small. We are all basically composed of the same stuff—mostly water and empty space, and the rest a loose structure of elements we have in common, all found on the same periodic table.

In fact, one could actually say the same of many inanimate objects! Of course living things, plant or animal, have exceptional additional qualities, such as the ability to reproduce.

Based on our understanding of physics, biology, and chemistry, there is no reason to separate any animals or plants in terms of basic composition. We even have trouble with our current system of categorization. Right off the bat, we usually think of an animal having a brain, eyes, mouth, etc. But creatures such as sponges or microorganisms such as amoebas challenge that notion. Some plants, such as the Venus flytrap, actually move more than some animals, such as a sponge. So drawing a line between animals and plants is complex enough, not to mention people and animals. A person like Jim is not convinced by these elements of scientific knowledge though—his view is based solely on one theological perspective—something founded only on belief instead of direct observation. This is obviously a mindset I do not share.

I can understand the criticism that our world should be packed to the brim with ghosts if we're to accept that every animal and/or plant may potentially produce one. This may sound like a great point to the uninformed, but the matter is simple to explain. If a phantom is indeed conscious and interactive then it must be able to choose, in some cases, the extent to which it can interact with our realm—or it's being forced to reside here according to some greater consciousness or plan beyond our usual grasp. I should also mention that, if reincarnation actually is a process of life, maybe we don't have tons of leftover spirits because they're constantly recycled back into our living realm (perhaps after a grace period).

If a phantom is some nonconscious residue from the past, either something that replays itself from time to time or something that can only be observed under the proper conditions, and maybe only by certain people, then we can expect these encounters on a limited basis. The manifestations occur at the whim of many variables, such as environmental conditions in the external world and the physiological/mental conditions of the observer. Of course, to be completely fair and accurate, we must keep in mind that there is ultimately no such thing as the "objective world." Even if 100 percent of the world population agrees on a fact, and each person has faith in a properly-calibrated instrument that can supposedly measure and confirm that fact, we're still left with the subjective impressions of people and the subjective interpretations of how those people's instruments function and detect. Nonetheless, for the purpose of systematically understanding any phenomenon, we can, and I do, use the term "objective" as appropriately as possible related to the opinions of most experts in a certain field of observation.

Perhaps you're seeing how complicated the subject of understanding ghosts can be. Quantum physics currently tells us that your brain doesn't necessarily know the difference between a daisy you imagine and a daisy you see in a field, also observable to others. In the same fashion, you probably can't tell the difference between something you experience daily and the world you inhabit during a dream at night. Reality ultimately occurs in your brain. And so drawing a clear, bold line between what is real and what is not real is impossible. This is our greatest challenge as paranormal investigators. Ghosts are mysterious, and therefore controversial, because they inhabit that broad, gray area, what others may ironically call a "fine line," between what observers experience as truth and what our current technology is able to effectively document. If we knew everything in the world, science would come to an end. As the realm of science rages with more enthusiasm than ever, it is obvious that there is much to learn—surely more than we can imagine. We therefore can't be too reliant on the measurements of our current tools while placing less emphasis on human perception. Indeed humans are also tools, complex and advanced enough to sense things unparalleled by our technology. Even as I write this, we currently do not have a device to match the ability of the human nose, capable of discerning from a wide range of aromas upon walking into a room. Some ghosts are only smelled and never seen or heard.

As this chapter proceeds, we will examine what an animal ghost may be—that is to say, of what an animal apparition may be composed. In doing so, I'll navigate those treacherous grounds between fact and fiction, science and belief, the real and unreal, as carefully as possible. All we can do is speculate, and yet we know more now than ever before in history. Part of the issue is understanding the materialization of specters in general, the other facet is looking at how animals specifically may fit into this platform. Even if humans and animals may both possess souls, there are still obvious differences between us and them, and it's important to be cognizant of how those variations might affect their nonphysical presences.

In the last chapter, skimming the recorded history of phantimals without scientific prejudice, I first divided these creatures into ghost animals (entities and imprints) and ghostly animals (elementals and harbingers). That system, more or less, labels the encounters according to phantimal behavior. But based on my experience investigating the paranormal in the field, evidence suggests that regardless of where a ghost fits on that table of experiences, it seems all phantoms manifest in one of two ways, or in a combination of both. For simplicity, we shall roughly call these internal and external encounters.

An internal encounter is perceived subjectively without any prospect of an objective presence. If the phantimal was not, or could not, be photographed, taped, or recorded in any physical medium, left no traces such as footprints or hairs, and was witnessed by no one else, it would fall into this category—something that we cannot separate from a hallucination. If two or more people have the same internal encounter, it pushes the experience more toward an external encounter, but it is still only internal.

The external encounter is one in which the phantimal can be, or is, photographed, taped, or recorded in any physical medium, left traces such as footprints or hairs, and was, or could be, observed by more than one person. If you're the only one to see the creature, but still gain physical evidence, then it will qualify as an external.

Determining definitions for ghostly activity is a very tricky business. We're looking at the nature of reality itself, and there are no ultimate answers. Nothing is ever certain. Remember that science is incapable of giving you truth, only theories founded on observations that should allow the prediction of certain outcomes. If you'd like a more detailed breakdown defining this sort of thing, I must humbly recommend my book, a practical guide, called *How to Hunt Ghosts* (Touchstone Books, 2003). But for our purposes, understanding the picture without training to become a paranormal investigator yourself, the broad terms of internal and external should suffice. Let us begin, however, by appreciating how reality itself seems to be constructed.

The Fabric of Reality

Everything is energy. That sort of statement is oft said, but seldom reflected upon intently. It seems almost like some kind of intangible concept describing something that exists no more than immeasurable emotions such as love and hate. And yet, don't emotions have a solid impact on the physical world, just as thoughts control the body? To honestly grasp the concept that everything is energy, it is essential to define *energy* or at least refresh the term if you've been out of school a while.

Energy is the ability to do work. *Work* is a change or transfer of force. Think of that for a bit—energy is not a physical object, but the capacity to produce change. Because everything is energy, that means our world is a swirling, oscillating, vibrating, interconnected body of development. In the most accurate sense, there is no such thing as physical or nonphysical. It is philosophically impossible for these two terms to co-exist in the universe if they interact. This dilemma is exemplified by the classic mind-body dilemma. The problem arises in determining how the mind, a supposedly nonphysical thing, can control the movement of the body, a supposedly physical thing. How could there be a point at which tangible and intangible meet? Those two interact because they are the same, only existing at differing frequencies. It's possible that the "mind" shedding the body is no different than you clipping a fingernail, or furthermore existing though your arms and legs are amputated. Perhaps you always exist to some degree, at some frequency, but your shape, size, and mass can change and transition as energy is transferred.

Two frequencies in the same general range can potentially resist each other, therefore creating the perception of what we call "physical" contact. Something seems physical to your body if it exists within the same frequency range as your body. We don't know exactly what those boundaries are, but look at yourself in relation to microwaves. You can't see or hear them, and so they are mainly intangible to you aside from how they affect your molecules (making them speed up). However, if your body were made of microwaves, you would be able to experience microwaves physically, just like liquid water or a chunk of rock. The idea of physical and non-physical is relative—the result of the extent to which one frequency range can, or cannot, interact with another. All energies may have the ability to affect all others to some degree, but that effect must be realized to be appreciated by humans. For example, ultraviolet rays from the sun could burn you 10,000 years ago as easily as today. But before humans understood ultraviolet rays, and gave them a name, those rays did not exist in the reality of mankind's worldview, only the rays' warming/burning effect. Because all reality is ultimately subjective, something does not fully exist until we truly acknowledge it.

When a phantimal is encountered, whether or not it is experienced internally, externally, or both, largely depends on the range of frequency at which it manifests. The exception, of course, would be a hallucination. Because a hallucination is generated by the mind, and can be anything, there's no sense in exploring it with this book—you'd best consult an expert psychologist on that one. So let's look at internal phantimal encounters assuming they are not the product of hallucinations. It may be impossible for us to ever actually know the difference, and that said, we must give equal weight to the possibility that these specific encounters have some external presence, undocumented as of yet, that could only be, or only was, observed internally.

Like all things, animals occupy a certain range of frequencies. Perhaps when they are alive to us, that range includes the part of the spectrum we call physical. When they die, they shift frequencies slightly, shedding that particular layer we experience physically, like a coat, but still existing to some degree at a different level. Though we presently have no way of scientifically analyzing this possibility, it is a potentially testable hypothesis nonetheless. We simply must learn how to register the particular energy fields associated with life in the non-physical state. The difficult part probably is not creating an instrument that is sensitive enough, but one that can filter out whatever special frequency range is associated with the state, distinguishing it from the infinite range of universal frequencies drowning it out in a cluster of powerful interference.

In the sprawling sea of energy oscillations, the electromagnetic medium of reality, it seems a large variety of creatures exist.

Some of them have never entered the realm of our perception, physical or otherwise. Others may only enter temporarily, such as the elemental black dogs that aren't like our normal, earthbound canines, yet are somehow related. And then we have creatures, such as our pets, who live a full life in our physical realm and then continue at a different frequency range after the physical life expires.

All this may sound fine from a broad, theoretical perspective, but how we can bring this subject down to Earth? By what proven mechanisms might a pet ghost manifest, regardless of how we classify it based on behavior and other characteristics? It is in addressing that question that some of our most significant breakthroughs have come, in recent years, regarding ghostly encounters.

Science is designed to help us solve the easiest mysteries first, the product of Occam's Razor. This is because the scientific method is based on observation. As a database is created over a period of observation, patterns and possible cause-effect correlations are noted. These are eventually used to create a testable hypothesis, hopefully leading to a theoretical solution. So the sooner those patterns and correlations are evident, the faster a mystery can be solved. But when the subject of activity occurs sporadically and rarely, the time needed to solidify a database in which patterns emerge is much greater. To a certain extent, a typical researcher must have faith in the potential reality of a subject to initially devote enough time to observation. Otherwise, the whole exercise could simply be a huge waste of time. It's all the more difficult when the subject of study, like a ghost, may possess consciousness and free will: the ability to be unpredictable and uncooperative. To draw conclusions, the scientific method is largely dependent on consistency—sometimes far too much to ask of nature. It also doesn't help that so many nonscientific people are attracted to mysterious subjects, broadly tainting the field of legitimate research.

Thanks to modern technology allowing a wider range of civilians the ability to measure a more extensive spectrum of energies, mainly because technology is cheaper and easier to manufacture (and more convenient to use in the field), the collective database has grown notably in the past couple decades. One of the best examples is the video camera. Not only are they compact and efficient, but the latest models have modes with enhanced sensitivity to the infrared realm. Infrared lies just below what we can see with the naked eye, at a lower frequency and longer wavelength. Because a camera can essentially capture what your eyes see, plus some ranges your eyes cannot see, it broadens your likelihood of documenting an anomaly simply because it altogether broadens the range into which you can see. As camera technology continues to develop, and we can visualize an even wider array of frequencies, I feel sure many paranormal phenomena will finally be understood.

In the late 20th and early 21st centuries, paranormal investigators like myself have collected the widest database of ghostly encounters in human history. This is not only due to the available field research technology, but also the ability to communicate on a vast level due to the Internet. Of course, the popularity of paranormal subjects in the media also helps immensely, giving us more access to paranormal sites since property owners have more open minds. By utilizing these benefits, we are now making important headway concerning what phantoms are and how they materialize. If we're lucky, we can one day find means of opening a portal that will allow beings in different energy realms to communicate with each other—a telephone system to other states of existence. This would enhance our consciousness enough to revolutionize our views of life, our place in the universe, and how we prioritize our ambitions.

Let's first look at ghosts that seem to be the entities of once-living pets. They match the most traditional and popular idea of a ghost—some spirit or soul that "comes back from the dead." When addressing this issue, we must first look at the living, physical body if we are to understand what aspects may potentially survive after death. It seems that whatever this ethereal form may be, our pets possess it in physical life, as well. Upon "death," it is merely the part that does not die.

Ghost Animals

In physical life, your pet has an electrodynamic body. This means the biological organism is a raging interaction of electrical impulses and magnetic fields along with chemical reactions. Any physical life-form churns with these characteristics and exists in a constant state of change. All physical reality can ultimately be reduced to electric and magnetic components. We directly envision our reality as a bunch of separate objects, however large or small, bumping against each other, moving according to Newton's laws. Though this is accurate at many levels, it is not absolutely accurate, as especially seen in terms of living things.

Every object around you does not have a clear, defined boundary of presence. Instead, each object is a cloudy mass, with clusters of even smaller particles tending to congregate at particular points. Observationally, it's the difference between viewing a photograph at one-thousand-times magnification and seeing a soft spread of blue and white dots, then pulling back significantly to view a grassy horizon distinctly against an azure sky. Every object relates to every other with this vague connection at the most intimate points of contact. Nothing is completely solid and, as previously noted, everything is mainly empty space.

When viewed at the microscopic level, the only difference between an inanimate object, such as your water glass, and your pet bird is the activity of the particles. The glass's atoms are always moving, but vibrate far less than those of what we call a living organism. The amount of energy an animal possesses is enormous by comparison. Living creatures burn with amazing electromagnetic energy.

The amount of energy organisms possess has been studied for many decades. We know for a fact that each time the heart beats, an electrical pulse passes through the body. Thousands of neurons can fire in the brain each second, producing a squiggling storm of charges. One of our most sensitive machines, the super conducting quantum interferometric device, also called a SQUID, documents this fire of activity. We also know that, according to the law of conservation of energy, energy can be neither created nor destroyed, simply transferred to another form.

When a pet dies, does the energy from his or her body disappear? Absolutely not! There is no doubt about that issue. The only question is: how does that energy continue? Does it simply dissolve and disperse like fine sands in the wind, spreading back to the universe without retaining any collective shape and history? Or does it indeed keep some of its prior form, perhaps even the memories and personality of the creature from whence it came? This is where controversy arises.

We cannot say, for a fact, that the energy of a dead creature does not simply distribute back to the cosmos and no organized remnant of that being remains. But there is good reason to explore the possibility that this is not the case. Aside from all the eyewitness reports of interactive, aware entities, we can also look to imaging.

Nikola Tesla was one of the greatest electrical geniuses who has ever lived. He once worked for Thomas Edison, and the two had a historic disagreement over whether commercial electricity should be delivered via direct current (DC), which remains steady, or alternating current (AC), which switches between positive and negative. Tesla, inventor of the AC generator, obviously promoted that form of delivery, and was especially impressed by the enormous amount of power that could produced using transformers to boost the AC current. Tesla is one of the first people in history to use electricity to create photographic images. By applying current to negatives, bolts of energy could be recorded even though the emulsion had not been exposed to light in the traditional manner.

The idea of making photographs with electricity was especially advanced in the 1940s and 50s by Russian researchers Semyon and Valentina Kirlian. They took various subjects, whether animate or inanimate, and passed electrical current through them while the subjects were pressed against

Photo courtesy of JoshuaPWarren.com.
Kirlian photo of a leaf in one of L.E.M.U.R.'S experiments.

a piece of film in a dark room. The resultant image showed a fiery aura of light, called a *coronal discharge*, around the matter being electrified. There is nothing paranormal about obtaining this kind of image. A coronal discharge is easy to observe with the naked eyes when a somewhat conductive object is charged with so much energy that some leaks off in a display of light, usually blue. This is often called St. Elmo's Fire, named so due to seamen observing the affect on a ship's topmasts during a thunderstorm, the product of clouds sweeping by and building up strong charges.

Artificially applying thousands of volts to a subject, in the dark, while lying against a piece of film, understandably gives us coronal discharge imagery. Today, the technique is known as Kirlian photography. But this type of imagery got extremely weird when the first reports of "phantom images" emerged using this technology.

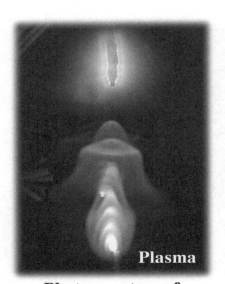

Plasma

**Photo courtesy of
JoshuaPWarren.com
A plasma in the lab, as created by
L.E.M.U.R. engineers.**

Basically, researchers would take a leaf and make a typical Kirlian photograph of it, displaying the glowing coronal outline. Then they'd tear away significant portions of the leaf and make another photograph on a separate photographic plate. This time the portions that were torn away would still appear glowing! This seemed to prove that even though the physical structure was destroyed, an energy structure continued to exist. A possible connection to ghosts is obvious.

To this day, the reality of the phantom Kirlian effect is still disputed. The concept has not yet been properly tested in a controlled setting. Those who claim to have obtained the effect say it's not easily repeatable—many variables such as atmospheric conditions, voltage and amperage, and the time the photo is made after the cut occurs must be considered. You might think that such an outstanding possibility is being adamantly researched by someone, but amazingly that's not the case—at least publicly. Though I myself am a rare owner of a Kirlian camera, even I don't presently have the resources to devote necessary time to properly testing this phenomenon to an extent resisting all scrutiny. Conducting Kirlian photography, done to the appropriate standards of scientific research, is a tedious endeavor. Critics understandably fault everything from the incompetence of the photographer to a variety of environmental elements, such as humidity, that can obscure exactly what is happening. But even though we can't say what's happening with absolute certainty, imagine if we are indeed proving that an energy structure remains even after a physical form deteriorates or is destroyed. This alone might account for why entities exist.

It's not uncommon for someone who loses a limb to speak of feeling it afterward. Sometimes the missing part hurts, itches, or tingles. Some doctors say this is only the imagination. *If*, however, it's another confirmation of the phantom Kirlian phenomenon, and all this evidence indeed proves true, imagine what it means! At the simplest, most basic level, it may be the foundation for how an object, and especially a living organism, can survive our perception of death. To some degree, this might explain how an aspect of your pet remains after a portion of it dies.

If some portion of your pet survives which is capable of conducting electricity, that would certainly explain many of the paranormal reports I've gotten through the years related to animal entities. These ghosts are often described as having a luminous quality, sometimes translucent, accompanying cold patches of air, and making hair stand on end. Such effects are most often reported when the air is dry and enhances static electricity, like when the charge built dragging your socks across carpet produces a shock from a metal doorknob. In the lab, my colleagues and I have been able to create many spectral effects, such as luminous, translucent light forms, cold spots, and hair standing, artificially by using electrostatic generators. Therefore, I think there's a connection between how some entities manifest and electrostatics. A strong electrostatic charge creates a 3-D light form made of *plasma*. Plasma is the fourth state of matter, produced when a gas, such as air, is exposed to so much energy that it becomes electrically conductive.

Perhaps a ghost somehow "uses" electrical charges in the air to manifest. Or it could be a phantom is always there, but can only be observed externally when enough free-floating charges are present at a particular place. Either way, such charges may provide the link between the observable and unobservable, just like how iron filings help us see a magnetic field. Though a magnet's field is invisible, if the magnet is held beneath a paper with iron filings sprinkled about, the filings adhere to the field, giving us a physical representation of the energy's form. Instead of iron filings, maybe a ghost's intangible form requires electrostatic charges to become physically interactive. After physical death, the form left over may be so subtle, in terms of our realm, that it requires an exceptional boost in environmental energy to become present to us again, and even then only on a very limited basis. This type of materialization would be considered external because it could potentially be photographed and audio recorded; those mediums are sensitive to electromagnetic signals.

If there's any validity to this, it would not only apply to interactive entities, but also imprints. There is no difference in imagining how a form's residual presence could transcend, and so separating an entity from an imprint would solely rely on our interpretation of the phantimal's behavior. An interactive and aware phantimal would be an entity, while a redundant, non-interactive, non-aware phantimal would be an imprint.

The possibility of imprints is more rooted in the mainstream sciences than perhaps any other form of phantimal. This is thanks to quantum physics. According to that discipline, we know time travel is possible. The rate of time flow varies all over the Earth. In fact, time passes faster on a mountaintop than at the bottom of the ocean because it goes slower closer to the Earth's center. It has been well-documented that time-flow alters with speed. Because we know for a fact that time is a flexible thing, we should accept that time is really just an illusion. There is no true past, present, and future. In a way, everything is happening at the same time and simply being experienced at different speeds by various observers and points of observation. Therefore, glimpsing into the past from time to time is to be expected.

We don't have the technology to build a machine capable of time travel, and we don't know how the human mind works. At the very least, our brains are just as complex as the universe itself because we are a direct product of the universe's craftsmanship. Perhaps we are perfectly capable of time traveling mentally by some means not yet fully understood nor close to our technology. One can imagine each of our brains as little time machines. The simplest version is exemplified by Einstein's famous quote when asked to explain relativity simply: "When a man sits with a pretty girl for an hour, it seems like a minute. But let him sit on a hot stove for a minute and it's longer than any hour. That's relativity." Who knows how drastically some observers can warp time?

An imprint might be the product of mental time travel, or some whim of the environment. Perhaps when atmospheric conditions are right, due to solar flares from the sun, passing comets, ocean currents, or any other huge variables (or a combination thereof) something from the past is replayed, like the information signature on an audio or video tape—a loop of information available for a long time after it exists, if not perpetually. It's conceivable that we'll one day have a machine, like a pair of goggles we wear to observe the past, tuning through the years like channels on a television.

Regardless of whether it's an entity or imprint, perhaps an externally observable ghost animal can affect its surroundings in two ways. First, by making traditional impressions on its surroundings, like leaving footprints, hairs, and damaged goods in its wake. Second, by triggering electrical anomalies such as strange illuminations, burns, levitations, and electronic interference. This is the result of a creature's aspect occupying our physical realm, however limited the basis, in the usual ways, but requiring an electrically-enhanced environment, and accompanying extraordinary side effects, to permit the interaction.

If the phantimal can only be observed internally however, that greatly reduces the chance of electrical effects accompanying the incident. In those cases, it may be that the phantimal exists in the very same variation, either entity or imprint. However, the conditions were not right for the ghost to shift into our physical frequency, and no electrical byproducts occur. Though we can't be sure if physical manifestations create the electrical anomalies, or such anomalies already existing in the environment facilitate the materializations (that is, the cause-effect relationship), we can only rest assured that, when a ghost becomes externally-observable, a paranormal electrical aspect is present. It seems a phantimal can be observed on an exclusive, internal basis if the particular observer is sensitive to the appropriate range—a range that science can't yet define.

It's well known that every person has a unique range of vision. Some of us see slightly more toward the higher frequencies, the ultraviolet realm, and others toward the lower frequencies, or infrared. I've heard anecdotes about the Allied forces experimenting with this subject during World War II. They supposedly were interested in creating airport runway lights that only certain people could see. Tests were done to see if light/dark eyes were consistently more sensitive to higher/lower frequencies. We can't say for sure whether the fact that some people can see a ghost while others cannot is dependent on vision-range sensitivity. That is one possibility, though.

Years ago, I signed at a book convention and a rather meek woman approached. "Can a blind person see a ghost?" she asked. I must admit, I was immediately thrown by the question, and only then realized the woman herself appeared to be sightless. My first instinct was to say, "No—but there are other ways to perceive ghosts, using audio recorders and meters." Then I began to think more about the grand question: where does vision occur, in the eyes or in the brain? Obviously, it occurs in the brain. How can I be so certain? Look at dreams.

I'm an avid dreamer—one of those folks who starts dreaming even before I'm fully asleep, and then right up past the moment I awake, in some cases. Those magnificent worlds I explore at night do not exist in front of my eyeballs, only in my mind's eye. In 2005, a wonderful report was published in the

Proceedings of the National Academy of Sciences scientific journal by researchers at the University of Houston, Texas. It confirmed the existence of "blindsight." As implied by the name, this is the phenomenon of blind people being able to see; in this particular case, when the eyeballs are fine, but there's damage in the pathway between them and the primary visual cortex. The scientists deactivated the vision of 12 normal subjects by beaming a special electromagnetic field into their heads. Even then, with no conscious usage of the eyes, the volunteers were still able to see shapes and color in front of them, correct beyond the probability of chance. They concluded a visual pathway bypassing the primary visual cortex must be responsible for blindsight.

When a phantimal is internally observed, that doesn't necessarily mean it's any less real than one externally present. This only means it's harder to document and it exists in a realm outside the physical, one that can only be observed by some people who have a natural ability, perhaps by some unusual characteristics of the eyes or brain, to perceive that realm. Because these kinds of phantimals don't achieve actual physical status, they generally seem more like normal animals. This is because they are not accompanied by the electrical anomalies of those who do become external.

As a side note, I should mention that some ghosts, whether entities or imprints experienced internally or externally, are not products of creatures that have died. Ghosts of the present and future are also seen. A ghost of the present would entail seeing your pet's spirit while your pet is still alive, but occupying a different location/position in space-time. A ghost of the future would be a spirit you encounter that later matches a physical specimen you meet. Exploring those ideas in particular can be laboriously speculative. However, both may be related to the fact that time, and our place in the property of time, is absolutely flexible. Such instances push forth the farthest boundaries of our research because they are, by far, the most difficult to investigate. Encounters with ghosts of the present/future usually only occur once, and are almost impossible to study scientifically right now.

Ghostly Animals

Elementals and harbingers are surely the most intriguing phantimals. For many, the idea of an elemental, in particular, is almost impossible to accept. Indeed, such hesitation to recognize, or enthusiasm to strongly criticize, the concept of elementals is completely understandable and consistent with scientific scrutiny. Even I find this category most difficult to rationalize, but that is only due to the human tendency to require familiarity for acceptance. Let me explain.

Believing a ghost may exist as representing some aspect of a creature that lived physically and then died is at least grounded in the fact the organism *did* live physically. It is therefore based on a premise we know, without reasonable doubt, to be true. The reality with which we are familiar consists of a fairly consistent process. A creature springs to life from another creature, however the mechanism for that species (for example, mammalian live delivery, eggs, asexual binary fission, and so on.). The organism grows over time, consuming energy, may reproduce, gradually weakens and deteriorates, and then dies—a predictable arc of events. Because we are intimately familiar with that routine, we generally expect every creature to, at very least, function to that extent in order to be real. And then we expect such organisms to be confined by our physical laws relating to gravity, movement of forces, thermodynamics, and such. But an elemental does not function that way at all.

An elemental seems to be almost immortal by our terms. It is a creature generally not of this physical world. It may share certain characteristics with normal animals—just as an alien from a distant planet may resemble humans insofar as having two arms, legs, and eyes, a general "humanoid" form—yet is vastly different in other ways. As opposed to being born, requiring energy, and dying as regular animals do, elementals seem to pop in and out of our realm quickly, and are not completely restricted by our physical laws. The bounds are endless. Devil dogs are definitely my favorite examples because they look so much like physical dogs in visible design, yet are extraordinarily huge, have glowing eyes, can perform amazing physical feats, and then vanish as quickly as they appeared.

It could be that elementals actually do live according to the biological arc we have in our realm. However, they live out most of this path in a different realm, at a different pace, and only seem immortal to us because we only observe them when they switch briefly in and out of this world. It may also be a popular misconception that elementals only come here to fulfill a certain mission, such as guarding something or exacting revenge. Perhaps we only pay enough attention to realize an animal is an elemental when it is performing these outstanding tasks. For all we know, many of the animals observed in the wild could be elementals, however unlikely.

We know that there are many other frequencies we consider nonphysical—infrared, microwave, radio, ultraviolet, X-ray, gamma ray—so is it not possible that other animals live, as real as us, but in those other frequency ranges? At times, if they are able to consciously or unconsciously lower/ raise their frequencies and/or we are able to consciously or unconsciously lower/raise ours, maybe we sometimes draw close enough for a physical interaction on a limited basis. Later, when addressing cryptids, we can explore even more what the proper conditions may be.

However this process may work, it's important to note the root of the term *elemental: element*. The primary definition of *element* is a fundamental, essential, or irreducible constituent of a composite entity. By simply calling such creatures elementals, we imply they are actually even more real than we are. We insinuate they are the most basic, durable, timeless components of life, and that we exist in a much more finite and temporal way. Of course, in pointing this out, I don't mean to suggest this is the case. I only emphasize that by historically identifying these beings by such a term, the subjective impressions of those who've experienced these phantimals are clear. All over the world, those who know elementals consider them to occupy a deeper level of reality than man; one that is perhaps closer to God or the Devil; one that carries primal meaning.

I recently interviewed Dr. Edgar Mitchell, the sixth man to walk on the moon, and founder of the Institute of Noetic Sciences, spearheading paranormal research. At one point, the subject of a possible sixth sense arose. Dr. Mitchell said perhaps we should not call it the sixth sense; it's actually the first sense from which the others developed. I found his perspective enlightening. In the same fashion, maybe elementals are beings somehow closer to the first sense, the fundamental layer of consciousness. If so, that might explain why so many cultures, for hundreds and thousands of years, have automatically concluded elementals exist on a powerful, ancient level. Perhaps when the observer's gaze strikes the piercing glow in a hellhound's eyes, a pang of heavy fear and wonder plucks deep in the person's bowels. Maybe it's a direct, instinctual response that leaves no doubt the elemental is archaic, tough, and wise.

A reasonable person should easily see that it's entirely possible for creatures to exist in a realm outside of what we call the physical realm. A slight stretch of the imagination can rationalize the possibility our dimensions can merge at times, bringing our realities together. Though there's no proof of this, all can be plausible according to what we know about how the world is composed. But there is one huge, glaring problem. To base this concept purely on speculation leaves the door wide open. We could just as easily invent a new animal—some glowing, balloon-headed, one-horned platypus that shoots lasers from its ear and eats rocks—and indeed have as much evidence for it as any other elemental, aside from eyewitness reports (which are so easily tossed away). This makes the concept of elementals decidedly unscientific, and yet that still does not deny the chance they may exist, as with anything else.

As you can see, to fully believe that elementals are real is to open yourself to an infinitely broad spectrum of possible creatures. These include fairies, trolls, mermaids, and the like, all of which, especially mermaids, can blur the line between humans and animals. I had a personal experience that seems relevant here.

For months, a friend of mine insisted I visit a scenic wilderness estate where fairies are reported. She herself had been taken there by some friends and observed tiny blue lights hovering in the air, meandering magically through the trees at night. I was finally able to make arrangements to go there myself. The owner confirmed, by phone, that these were fairies, beings from another dimension, and they only come around at a certain time during summer. I was invited to visit and freely observe them for myself.

I was told the "fairies" mainly appeared around a particular garden. At twilight I relaxed on a secluded stone bench, surrounded by twisting masses of finely manicured vines, a plethora of sweet-smelling flowers, and bubbling fountains. Once the sun fully sank, the forest darkened, and the sky was a light shade of deep purple, my eye caught the first twinkle in the woods. As you can imagine, I hardly believed it, and raced off into the woods for a closer look. The light twinkled again on its route through the trees, appearing and disappearing between the black silhouettes of growth. After nearly killing myself in bushes, on mossy stones, and on slippery inclines, the critter was inches away from my face. At that point, I clearly saw the "fairy" was nothing more than an unusual firefly. Fireflies, or lightning bugs, are common in those parts that time of year, but the insects usually blink. This one flew slowly and cast a slight yellowish glow constantly, never blinking. It was a curious creature, but not a fairy by my standards. So I made my way back to the garden still hoping to see a real fairy.

When I returned, the desolate spot I'd left was now packed with a group of people—regular fairy-watchers, who'd congregated in my absence. Most were women, and they were surprised when a man came trudging from the evening woods. The shadowy group asked what I was doing and I said "Oh, I just saw a light in the woods over there and ran for it. But it was just a lightning bug of some sort." They sort of dismissed what I'd said in a funny, arrogant way and turned their attention elsewhere. I sat back down on the bench.

A few minutes later, we beheld an enchanting sight. Now that it was much darker, a swarm of small lights, just like what I'd observed, slowly emerged from the trees. It was like a tiny galaxy before us, pinpoints of illumination spread around. The women were awestruck. "Look at all the fairies tonight!" they exclaimed, completely ignoring me. I sat back to listen, and soon realized these insects, just like the one I observed closely, were their "fairies." I started to snatch one in my hand to show them we were only looking at bugs. But then I thought better. For one thing, if I'd been disrespectful enough to catch one, I feel quite sure they'd have killed me for heresy. Secondly, it would be egotistical for me to ruin their fun, at that moment, under those circumstances, by playing the devil's advocate. Thirdly, I began to feel a sense of eeriness being alone deep in the woods with a bunch of people who may be insane enough to call bugs "fairies." And so I left with that.

Either fairies look a lot like little, black insects, or the other observers wanted to believe in fairies so much that these bugs were interpreted as such. Making this transition in thought may be greatly enhanced by one rare variation exhibited: the lack of blinking among adults of this particular, and perhaps unique, isolated species. And yet, there was one other thing about the experience I find perplexing. To me, each of the lightning bugs had a yellowish glow. But on numerous occasions, the women described it as being blue. Yellow and blue are not far apart on the visible spectrum, only separated by green (which can be made in paints by combining yellow and blue). Because I didn't have feedback from another male, I can't say for certain whether most men see yellow while most women see blue, or if I observed a different color for some other, and perhaps unrelated, reason. Maybe instead of the color difference being the product of male vs. female sight, it was the product of believer vs. nonbeliever sight. And I can't say with any certainty that my vision was correct while theirs was not. Perhaps it was just the opposite. Consider the possibility that my familiarity with fireflies distorted my perception of what was really there: a little, flying person, with a glowing aura, from another dimension.

I find this experience relevant because it plainly demonstrates part of the challenge when dealing with elementals. *To me, the creatures were primarily insects.* Yet I did not try to capture one because they not only appeared so clearly as insects without doing so, but because the uncontrolled environment did not practically yield itself to scientific investigation due to the social factors present. *To others, the creatures were primarily not insects.* They did not try to capture the creatures because their minds already seemed made up. I should give them the benefit of the doubt by saying that, perhaps, in the past they had been skeptical, captured one, recorded characteristics to convince themselves the beings are fairies, and therefore felt no need to redundantly proclaim their findings to me, an intrusive stranger in the dark. So I can't say for certain due to these variables impeding science. But the fact they saw a different colored light than me could be most telling of all. Whatever these creatures were, I experienced them differently than those around me, and the extent to which I considered them normal, and others considered them paranormal, is warped by the gray shrouds of defining our reality and the elemental.

The idea of a witch or sorcerer having a supernatural pet called a familiar may be rooted in elemental lore. Typical familiars, especially in European lore, have been cats, bats, a variety of birds, wolves, snakes, and frogs or toads. Those who prefer a more magical bent sometimes think the sorcerer can actually transform him or herself into the familiar. But a more common belief is that familiars are elementals that could only be tamed by a witch because such a goal is beyond the means of an ordinary mortal, unassisted by dark arts. This is partly because magicians, like vampires, have been envisioned with hypnotic powers, the ability to nefariously control and manipulate others. The strongest example would be an ability to tame an elemental—a creature of such ancient, powerful will—to perform one's bidding. Also phantimals, as well as psychic pets in general, are often described as having shiny, penetrating eyes. This matches well with the fear of "the evil eye," a belief that eyes are such direct windows to consciousness that a being can curse you with a sharp gaze, connecting you straight to its wish of ill will. Belief in the evil eye has been so strong that thousands of years ago Mediterranean sailors would paint huge eyeballs on ships to ward off and deflect negative energy. To this day, many in that culture, especially Turkey, still wear glass eye pendants for the same reason.

I've always found it interesting that so many animals can identify a living being based on the fact it has eyes. Though a scarecrow is a good, obvious example, similar dummies are employed every day in a variety of ways, always emphasizing the eyes. Actually, many of these scarecrows are simply balloons with nothing but big, flamboyant peepers painted on the surface. Isn't it amazing that a wild creature can't differentiate a living animal from a nonliving if the eyes are prominent enough?

Lastly, *harbingers* are unique in our classification of phantimals. A harbinger could be a nonphysical creature, an elemental, or a completely normal, physical animal that is fulfilling a specific mission. They are animals that appear in conjunction with a situation, almost as if the creature heralds the event, is attracted to it, or plays some other role we do not understand. Though a witch's familiar could be an elemental, especially if the beast possesses seemingly supernatural properties such as the ability to breathe fire, familiars may also be regular animals under a magician's spell. A typical example is a sorcerer who persuades an owl to fly miles away and drop a cursed stone on someone's house, fulfilling a spell, or a crow that slips in an open window to steal wisps of hair from someone's brush, allowing the witch to use the hair in a magical ceremony or voodoo doll. In these cases, the harbinger would be a direct participant in the event and responsible for the event.

In other cases, the harbinger may not cause the event, but simply be attracted by it. A good example may be the swarms of flies packed around some haunted houses. This type of incident, frequently reported, was popularized in *The Amityville Horror* by Jay Anson. The famous book, supposedly based on some true facts surrounding a haunting in New York State, recounts the first time George and Kathy Lutz, house owners, realized the abundance of insects near a room's foul stench:

> On this window, clinging to the inside of the panes, were literally hundreds of buzzing flies!
>
> "Jesus, will you look at that! House flies, now?"
>
> "Maybe they're attracted by the smell?" Kathy volunteered.
>
> "Yeah, but not at this time of year. Flies don't live that long, and not in this weather. And why are they only on this window?" George looked around the room trying to see where the insects had come from...
>
> "If this closet wall was up against the bathroom, they might have lived in the warmth. But this wall's against the outside." George put his hand against the plaster. "It's cold in here. I don't see any way they could have survived."

When a movie based on the book was remade and released in 2005, George Lutz conducted a fresh interview on the film's official Website www.AmityvilleHorror.com. He was asked about the reality of the fly plague:

> In the house, when we were there...the flies were almost always present in the second floor rear bedroom...we would kill them all and they would yet return and be there the next day or the next time we were in the room. This was a room we had set up as a sewing room for Kathy...I should add this was December/January.

A similar fly infestation has been experienced by the Jackson family of Lancaster, South Carolina. For nearly 10 years their property, an Indian torture ground long ago, has been extremely haunted by dark forces. Though the place is a rescue for a wide variety of animals, the flies do not congregate near the barn, but inside the Jackson home. In a written account detailing her experiences, owner Lynn Jackson said:

> *Then there are the flies. This is another sign of a haunting, if you see a lot of flies in your home or outside wanting to get in. You may see them hanging around your doors, windows or even in just the area that's haunted. This will even happen in the wintertime when flies are supposed to be dead. At one time, I went into my husband's master bathroom to put up some towels, the room seemed normal...I left the room for only a moment and came back to get my hairdryer. To my surprise there were about a hundred flies in the room. They were everywhere. I quickly ran and grabbed our fly swatter and started killing every one of them...I always have had a problem with the flies all over my front windows and doors. This was happening even in the coldest winters. They were making a mess out of everything by leaving behind their dark markings and we were all the time having to kill them when they would sneak their way inside our home. Before I linked them to the spirits, I couldn't figure out why they wanted inside instead of wanting to hang around where the farm animal's droppings were.*

Even more chilling, the Jackson farm was also plagued by spiders as Lynn recorded:

Another thing I was starting to notice was this place was filled with thousands of spiders, mostly black widow spiders and flies. Adam [her son] was even bitten by a small black widow. I had to take him to the hospital to get checked out. Amber [her daughter] has been bitten by several different types of spiders, some I've never seen before. She's been in the hospital about 5 different times due to spider bites from out here. One spider that bit her I was able to kill and take to the hospital with me so the doctors could see if he was a poisonous spider or not...the doctors told me they didn't know what kind of spider he was. They had never seen one like it before.

Many insects have an uncanny ability to locate dead bodies from miles away. Within minutes of death, flies in particular can seek out a corpse and begin laying eggs. The ability of insects to find dead flesh is so reliable that forensic investigators use the type and status of bug infestations to form a time line of death. Are these creatures simply smelling the aromas of cessation—the gases that start to release? Or is something else drawing them, perhaps an energy we don't yet fully understand?

If there is a mysterious energy that accompanies death, it may account for why insects are drawn to an area even though no rotting flesh is present. Maybe the decayed matter is long gone, but the energy is pervasive, lasting much longer, even pooling permanently at some places on Earth that are more conducive to contact with the deceased. It is easy to draw a connection between corpse-devouring insects and harbingers attracted to morbid hauntings. But harbingers can come in any form, including animals that do not usually seek out the dead. Therefore, perhaps flies are one type of harbinger, targeting one especially negative form of energy.

Because harbingers can be virtually any type of animal, we can't conclude anything specific about the relationship between a creature and a particular energy to which it is drawn. But it may be that even though we haven't classified the wide spectrum of paranormal energy types, each type, when concentrated enough, does potentially attract an animal. This view may easily explain the idea of omens: some symbol of a coming event.

Ancient Romans viewed owls as omens of disaster. Yet they chose to harness the power of owls and keep them nearby, in cages, to combat the evil eye. This can be easily understood given an owl's famously large, gleaming eyes and subsequent sense of intelligence. In a mix of cultures, including the Old South in the United States, finding a bird or bat in your house signifies a death that will soon occur amongst the residents. The same outcome is expected if a bat is seen flying in circles around a house three times. However, a wild bird flying straight toward you is thought to bring good luck. A cricket in the house can bring good or bad luck, depending on the culture.

There is some kind of superstition attached to almost any animal you can imagine in some culture somewhere. The lack of consistency from culture to culture can be seen as evidence against the objective reality of harbingers if that animal is supposed to be naturally attracted to a kind of energy. That's why harbingers have most often been thought of not as creatures seeking an attractive element, like a snake warming itself in the sun or a hummingbird drawn to sugar water, but as creatures who were, themselves, specifically charged as messengers or carriers—fulfilling a deed, as a witch's familiar.

The idea of a harbinger is complicated by a number of variables. First we have the possibility of it being a phantimal that simultaneously occupies a normal, physical existence. Next we have the question of whether or not these beasts appear in conjunction with a certain type of event because they're attracted to some energy signature of that event, or if they actually cause the event to occur by delivering the incident in some way. And lastly we have the difficulty of interpreting the possible role in relation to a significant incident that occurs. Was it a harbinger of good luck, bad luck, or was its presence entirely coincidental altogether, at least having no direct correlation to the incident of significance. There is no way to answer these questions with our current level of knowledge and data. It would take a long time, and much skilled, diverse labor to study these possibilities, and even then we probably could not reach a solid conclusion because humans are the ones who ultimately assign meaning to symbols, and on a wide scale humans can rarely agree on anything.

Because it's so difficult, if not impossible, to measure certain human responses and interpretations scientifically, it's all the more valuable to have the vocalized impressions of people who've encountered phantimals. After all, the human body is a type of meter—an antenna sensitive to energy we don't understand, exemplified by the fact we don't comprehend much about the human body, including that key element, the mind-body connection. A long history of phantimals is well-established. Now that we've tackled speculation on how and why they might manifest, let's put things in modern perspective and explore accounts of those that have been experienced recently, often straight from the people who experienced them.

3 Personal Experiences with Pets

Phantasmal Felines

Years ago, my skill as a paranormal investigator was tested. I, and a couple colleagues, accepted an invitation from an elegant widow named Cynthia. She lived in a venerable old Tennessee mansion, towering beside a crisp lake, in a wealthy community. Having traveled widely, always paying attention to the most mysterious sites on her journeys, she was a lifelong fan of paranormal pursuits. In her telephone introduction, she said her home was haunted by the soul of her dead husband and details would come when we saw her in person.

Upon arriving at the place, Cynthia greeted us warmly, hot cookies and cold milk waiting. Though we were sensitive to the supposed matter at hand, a dead spouse, she seemed in wonderful spirits. The volumes of dog-eared books packed on every table and shelf—about topics like pyramids, chakras, abductions, and séances—bore testament to her serious interest in the unknown. After a while engrossed in general conversation about ghost research, we were prepared to collect details regarding her haunting. But surprisingly, she seemed rather flippant about her husband's spirit. In fact, we later joked that she'd killed him. Instead, the objects of her fascination were two small apparitions prancing about the tall structure. She believed these were her two beloved cats.

Maximilian and Carlota were robust manx cats—the tailless kind. Cynthia would cuddle up with them at night, and spend each day as their playful mother figure. It was these cats who helped Cynthia recover after the loss of her husband from a stroke. And so, when Maximilian and Carlota died, the blow was devastating to say the least.

Max finally passed away from old age, and a saddened Carlota soon after contracted a severe upper respiratory infection that claimed her life. Losing them both in less than a year sent Cynthia into deep depression, especially after her husband was gone. She meditated on the essence of her pets, fueled by tales in spiritualist pulp books, and said the more she was aware, and openly invited their spirits to return, the more prominent the feline specters became.

In the beginning, Cynthia would hear her deceased pets meowing, or their soft feet occasionally misstepping in the house, a precariously placed object tumbling to the floor. Most comforting of all was when their purrs, in stereo unison, would join her in bed at night. And then, finally, an apparition appeared. Max was the first to materialize. He was a shadowy form visible in the living room for a few seconds on a summer evening. Two months later, as the chill of fall approached,

Carlota manifested. That night was stormy, "perfect for a visitation," she recalled, and "Carly couldn't have been more than a couple of feet away. She glowed slightly, greenish-blue, just like what you'd expect from a ghost."

In seeing the felines, Cynthia was most struck by how similar the animals looked to their living state, despite the aura about Carlota. It was a big deal for her to catch a glimpse of them, and yet they didn't look surprised at all that she could see them. It appeared the cats' perceptions had never really changed. They evidently could always see their owner as plainly and normally as in life. The familiar appearance of the cats' phantasmal forms made Cynthia feel all the more comfortable with them, and her own perception of what happens after physical death. "They looked," she paused, then chuckled, "shockingly normal."

Upon hearing her story, I immediately felt it was possible that Cynthia, in a state of deep distress, needed her beloved pets so much that she caused herself to hallucinate. Her indulgence in spiritualist literature may have provided a blueprint upon which her imagination was understandably built. This suggestion in no way demeans her overall psychological stability because this may simply be a natural side effect of deep mourning, by oneself, when surrounded by death and loneliness. But then, she surprised us.

"I want to know I'm not crazy," she said. "And I don't want to influence what you find, so we'll know the truth for sure." Yes? "And that's why I'm hoping you can use your equipment to prove that Max and Carly are here."

I explained to Cynthia that it's currently impossible to prove a ghost exists, only to prove that physical phenomena occur in conjunction with her experience of the phantoms. "That's why I want to experiment," she said. Cynthia explained that even though her manxs were usually around her, they had their own room. It was in this room that both Maximilian and Carlota died. "I'm sure there's some kind of energy there," she stressed, "and I bet you can find it. I won't tell you which room it is, and I want you to find it."

Being a mansion, the structure had plenty of rooms on several stories. Nonetheless we pointed out that, regardless of our results, there may be other cues to give away the room. Aside from a buildup of cat hairs, perhaps accompanied by a sudden allergy attack, maybe scratch marks, more impressions in the carpet, or mere location could subliminally sway our opinions. But Cynthia was not bothered by this situation. She said her pets had so much energy that whatever they left behind should be prominent and undeniable. At that, we set out. A variety of meters, sensitive to a variety of energies, were employed. Later I'll describe how investigation equipment works. But for now consider we were mainly testing for electromagnetic and electrostatic anomalies.

Less than a minute into the investigation, I stooped down to gain a control reading of the living room floor. To my surprise, the device registered a massive spike in energy. It was fleeting, so I blew it off. But as we made our way around the house, we consistently documented low-lying fields, unpredictably transient, moving around. The level, that is to say height, of the fields was, sure enough, the same as the height of an average cat. Cynthia had a slight grin, quietly watching us begin to glow with thought, scratching our heads as we discussed the odd fields.

Room by room, twisting staircase by staircase, we navigated the extremely neat and spacious house. At last we entered one room with a few odds and ends. Instantly, my colleagues and I looked to each other. Our devices registered pools of inexplicable, undulating energy near the floor. After a few minutes, we sat down on the carpet to continue our work. Eventually, even without researching the rest of the house, we told her it must be the room we'd sought. Beaming, Cynthia declared us exactly right. The space had been modified in various ways since the cats had passed there almost two years before. Nonetheless, in addition to the small, transient fields of compact energy flitting around the abode, there was something in that room which apparently did not leave—perhaps an imprint left there from all the emotion, both happy and sad, attached to the place for so long. It was a rewarding time for everyone present.

That case exemplified some of the most outstanding aspects of pet ghost manifestation. For one thing, such ghosts usually only manifest if they have an exceptionally strong emotional connection to the human owner. This is understandable because that bond is what apparently enhances the energy necessary, plus what makes a conscious entity want to be with the beloved owner. Plus, this tendency for a pet to come back is enhanced by the animal's relationship with other pets, left behind. This is especially outstanding when the animal is half of a couple, as with Maximilian and Carlota. Also, the length of the pet haunting seems to depend on the desire of the owner. If a person desires the spirit to stay, vocalizes that wish, and reinforces it on a daily basis, the phantom can remain indefinitely. But if the pet is told to move on, or is gradually ignored, the activity fades away. Keep these factors in mind as we explore more encounters with pet ghosts.

A Dog Who Followed From the Grave

Nick Redfern is an expert at separating fact from fiction. He's been a professional journalist for decades, and is the author of numerous books including Three Men Seeking *Monsters: Six Weeks in Pursuit of Werewolves, Lake Monsters, Giant Cats, Ghostly Devil Dogs and Ape-Men.* Born in England, he only moved to the United States several years ago, and was raised among the wealth of strange creature reports from the United Kingdom. You've probably seen him on television many times: a tall, slim, bald fellow, rather young, who speaks with articulate, encyclopedic knowledge. He's one of the few researchers who is well-rounded, having done considerable work on nearly every aspect of paranormal reports, all the while measuring his opinions carefully and skillfully based on facts.

We recently worked on a television project together and, in casual conversation, I was delighted to learn he had personally experienced a pet ghost. "As a hopefully grounded author and researcher, I truly don't, for one minute, believe it was my imagination or some unconscious comfort factor trying to make things easier," he said. The incident happened two years prior, and Nick's memory was clear. His wife, Dana, had owned Charity, a shar-pei ("one of the wrinkly dogs," he added) for eight years. Nick enjoyed the pet's company for three years of that time, and he described her as a "gentle, quiet dog with a kind of unique, funny character—very clever—she knew a lot of words."

Nick and Dana shared a Texas home with Charity, and the serious trouble began just a few weeks before they were moving to another town. After a mostly healthy life, she began displaying symptoms of joint pain after a run in the park. Visits to the vet promised optimism, but the dog's condition slowly deteriorated with time. They would eventually learn Charity suffered from familial shar-pei fever, a hereditary condition that not only includes joint pain and accompanied physical distress, but can produce bouts of sudden fevers up to 107° F (41.7° C). The Redferns did everything possible to save Charity from her morbid fate, but one afternoon the inevitable call came from the vet's office. Charity had died suddenly. She didn't even have a heart attack, the heart simply stopped beating. Needless to say, Nick and especially Dana were distraught.

They drove to a place called Pleasure Island, where Dana's father owns property, for a burial. The shallow grave was completed with a headstone: *Here lies our faithful friend and companion.* As they began the sad drive home, the weather turned sour, and hard rain poured from a dark sky. Passing the small, fresh grave, Dana, a firm believer in life after death, spoke out to her lost pet. "Come with us Charity! Don't stay here where it's cold and wet, follow us home!" Nick echoed the sentiment.

When back at their house, Nick entered the garage to deal with some laundry. He suddenly stopped in his tracks and called for his wife. "There was this overpowering odor of wet-dog smell," recalled Redfern. "If you can imagine a smell having solidity to it, that's what it was like; the most overpowering dog smell you can imagine." Both marveled at the powerful aroma, and for the first time wondered if Charity truly had followed them back home.

In the coming days, the outstanding dog smell would re-occur at various points around the house, seeming transient in nature. But that was just the beginning. Next they noticed a more tangible sign of the spectral visitor. After Charity's death, they'd vacuumed the living-room carpet thoroughly, smoothing out the dog's favorite spot to lie down. And yet, again and again, the distinct impression of a shar-pei formed in the floor, and the Redferns had no other pet.

On at least three occasions, Dana heard small claws click-ing on the house tiles. It sounded exactly like the shar-pei's small feet meandering down the corridor heading toward their bedroom. Charity commonly traversed that path in life, sometimes leaping on the bed to awaken her owners. What-ever weight imprinted the living room carpet was apparently moving distinctly around the house floors, as well.

Nick remembered having a dream about Charity so outstand-ing that it may have been an actual visitation. The shar-pei ap-peared along with Nick's old pet from England, a deceased cairn terrier named Susie. "It seemed very vivid," he said, "almost like I was awake. I had a feeling of them jumping on the bed. Their bodies felt very solid." Susie seemed composed, like a guiding old soul, and Charity was boisterous, excited to be back. Right before the encounter, Nick had the impression of a doorbell or knock to signify their entrance. He found this notable because, after interviewing so many people in his work, that same impres-sion was frequently recounted by those who claimed visits from spirits: there was a sense of the presences distinctly marking their entrances with something like a traditional knock.

These phenomena continued for weeks as the Redferns' moving deadline grew closer. Comforted by the company of their short, spectral friend, Dana in particular became more melancholy about leaving the spirit behind. Eventually, their last day in the house arrived January of 2004. All possessions were cleared, the mouth of a huge moving truck still gaping nearby. Dana took a moment to sit alone reflecting on the operation, ensuring all items were truly transferred. Though each physical object was preserved, she couldn't keep her mind from turning to Charity's spirit. Dana mentally invited the beloved canine to come along, and at one point during meditation realized, surprisingly, that one of Charity's hairs was stuck to the tongue of her shoe. Beside it, as a slogan on the shoe, was printed the words "Get a Move On." A warmth spread over her as Dana took this to be a message: it's okay to move on.

Photo courtesy of Nick Redfern,
Charity, the shar-pei who came back from the other side.
This is the actual photo Redfern found in the cupboard.

During his last examination of the house, making certain nothing had been overlooked, Nick felt confident each speck had indeed been retrieved. Every drawer was empty, each room barren. The last space of his investigation was a bedroom he'd converted to a study. He glanced inside a corner cupboard, seeing nothing. But as he almost turned to leave, being as thorough as possible, Nick jumped for a better look at a shelf several inches higher than his head. Something small and black caught his eye. With another pounce, he retrieved the tiny item. It was the negative of a photograph of—yes, you guessed it—Charity. As Nick recounted, "The one thing left in the house was this picture. It was almost like a message saying 'I'm not being left behind. I'm coming with you.' This was sort of like a synchronistic thing, or symbol to me, her way of getting the message across: you found me and I'm not gonna be left."

Charity's photo appearing in such a way, under those circumstances, was of great comfort to the Redferns. This was compounded when one of Nick's friends, a guy who spends a lot of time in Tibet, said he'd blessed a khata for Charity. Khatas are sacred prayer cloths in the Tibetan culture. Only later did the friend learn Charity was a shar-pei, and he found it truly fitting, given the breed's origin in Asia. These events brought closure to Nick and Dana. Afterward, they did not experience the pet's presence again. She had apparently moved on.

> *"There's absolutely no doubt in my mind that the initial week or 10 days after she died, some very, very weird things did happen," Nick reiterated. "After that immediate period things go quiet...the life force moves on, that's the impression we got. To*

this day, we haven't wanted another dog because we still miss her." Nick is often asked what he learned overall from the experience. "I truly do believe that her life force, in some capacity, was around. Not obviously being in a physical form, but that was her way, as with a lot of spirits, of getting the message across. Smells, imprints, weird dreams, coincidences, to say 'Hey, I'm still here, and do what you've gotta do and move on with your life.'"

As a person who has studied cryptids, like the devil dogs of England, I asked Redfern if they might somehow relate to the phantimal they encountered. The researcher sees a distinct difference between a normal canine ghost, such as Charity's, and such elementals, yet he's still very puzzled by them and trying to understand how the two may relate. Even the black dogs themselves behave inconsistently with each other. "They very often fall into two categories. One: if you see them and it's a helpful friend. People see them when they're walking down a lonely road; the dogs are perceived as some sort of guardian spirits. In other reports they're seen as a precursor to a death in the family or some kind of looming tragedy." In the case of Charity, her presence was either an entity or imprint—not at all what we think of when exploring the black dogs of Europe.

The Redfern experience stands out because their ghost never manifested visually, the classic idea of how a spirit returns. The closest may have been Nick's dream. And yet Nick and Dana still felt confident their pet had survived death and communicated with them through synchronistic events. Because we don't think of a dog having such ability even in life, does this imply that pets gain more intelligence on the other side? Or at least more ability to control circumstances around them? Or does some greater power in the universe simply speak on their behalf, ensuring the message gets across? We can't say for certain. But the connection between the owners and the pet clearly transcends their physical coexistence, and can certainly produce physical effects in our realm.

The Pork of Christmas Past

(*The names have been changed to protect the privacy of those involved.)

I've lived in a rural setting my whole life. The economy has often been troubled here in the past. In fact, Asheville, North Carolina, was supposedly hit harder than any other city in the United States, per capita, during the Great Depression. Many residents of these worn, blue mountains have relished a fresh slaughter as a godsend. It shouldn't be surprising that tales of barnyard animal ghosts abound. One of the more interesting incidents began with a hog named Gabriel. His name was chosen to represent his ultimate sacred purpose. Gabriel had been groomed for a long time: a fat, tasty prize for any dinner table, but especially on Christmas day.

Roy Shelton was a grizzled fellow whose family had been largely self-sustained for generations. He owned a sizable lot of property in Yancey County, one of the more remote sections of these parts. Roy and his siblings had grown up with pens of hogs, sheep, and foul, fields of grazing cattle, and he knew very well how to kill, skin, treat, and eat. But when, in his early 20s, he married Becca, a surprisingly wealthy woman from Atlanta, she demanded a change in lifestyle. "We don't live in 1920 and we're not poor," she'd say. "I can drive to the grocery store in 10 minutes. So we don't need all these filthy, stinking animals." So she put a stop to the idea of keeping and handling livestock. Roy begrudgingly obeyed her wishes, never exposing her and their children to those "barbaric" facts of life. His only opportunity to kill was on an occasional hunting trip, mainly for small game, and those excursions outcast him from the family a bit. However, all that changed after September 11, 2001.

After watching terrorist attacks in New York City and Washington D.C., shocked by the horrified, fleeing faces, Roy was immediately struck by the warnings of his grandparents—tales of the stock market collapse in 1929, hunger and poverty, eventually leading to the terrible World War II. Without hesitation, he knew 9/11 was his cue to make sure his family was well-fed and protected. Expecting the country to possibly descend into another dark era, he told his wife that, like it or not, he was raising some food on the land. Roy hoped she'd actually get used to it after a few years, and maybe even be proud of his capable hands. Though Becca didn't like the idea, she reluctantly agreed, being equally shocked by the nation's condition and paranoia of those around her.

One of Roy's first purchases was Gabriel, a fine little pig. It would take around 12 months of careful feeding to ensure the pig grew to a healthy, delicious state for a wonderful holiday meal. Roy especially took pride in teaching his 15-year-old son, Ruben, about the process. But he was slightly bothered by watching the boy pet and socialize with the animal. After all, a happy porker, its tail wagging, is a funny, friendly sight, and a young person can become attached quickly. The father was always quick to remind Ruben how mean a hog could be, and how powerful its jaws, and sharp its filthy teeth, were. "See this," Roy would say as Gabriel chomped a corncob in half with almost no effort. "Imagine that's your hand. And hogs eat people all the time," he halfway chuckled.

Eventually, as the holidays approached, Roy felt the time to slaughter Gabriel was about right. The animal had grown to a fine, fat beast, perfect really. As fate would have it, the day before Roy had decided to kill the hog, his employer, a lumber company, sent him on the road for an important, unexpected delivery. So he put off the slaughter till his return. But the delivery took him deep into the mountains of West Virginia, and the night he arrived, a blizzard swept down from the north and was on his heels. Not sure how many days his return would be delayed, he called Becca. "Tell Ruben where to find my .38 and get things started. I'll take over when I get back." Roy felt confident the boy could proceed because he'd spent months involving his son in the planning. But Becca protested loudly, knowing how fond of the pig their teenage son had become. Roy held his ground firmly. "For years, you've had your way with this issue. And now it's time to give. Ruben knows what to do, and he'll be a more secure adult knowing how to care for himself if necessary." She felt terrible after the call—for she had grown fond of Gabriel. But she nonetheless retrieved Roy's .38 pistol from their bedside, gave it to Ruben, and repeated Roy's words.

A part of the teenager was immediately excited. He knew how to use a pistol as his father had him popping off cans and cardboard boxes at an early age. But he'd never killed an animal, and he saw the glean in his father's eyes each time the prospect of a glorious, fresh ham for Christmas was discussed. The household was somber as Ruben walked outside to complete the deed. When he got to the stall and Gabriel came trotting over, tail wagging, a smile almost visible on his pink lips, Ruben's stomach sank a bit, and a veil of sadness overcame him, colder even than the air around him. His father had told him about the natural hesitation to kill a creature one has known for months. But he also made it clear that if the family were starving, there would be no hesitation, and this was practice for such a run. It was extremely important, and the duty gave Ruben a sense of importance, made him feel like a man.

He knew there was no sense in thinking about it, and so Ruben slowly raised the pistol, aimed carefully for a high spot between Gabriel's eyes, and fired. The shot cracked the air, and through the thin, drifting smoke there stood the hog, frozen, the bullet "wadded up," slightly embedded on his forehead. Time seemed to stop as Ruben and Gabriel stood silently, looking at each other.

They say a pig is very intelligent, even more so than a dog. And that intelligence can be seen most easily in the creature's eyes. This is why pigs have often been sacrificed by cults in place of humans. Pigs can be quite expressive, and at that particular moment, the smile was gone forever from Gabriel's mouth. His gaze was steady, stunned and icy cold, but his right eye was now cocked slightly to the inside, apparently rocked in his skull. The two simply stood quietly, each like a statue sharing a stony moment of confusion switching quickly to realization of what was happening. With that, Ruben experienced his first emotion since pulling the trigger: a small shudder ran down his spine and weakened his knees. He started to fire again, the only thing he knew to do, but his arm was now numb and like jelly. After a pause, dropping his head in brief reflection, Ruben simply turned and walked soundlessly back to the house. Behind him, Gabriel still stood in the stall, not moving an inch, his crooked eyes still locked. We will never know exactly what was in the hog's mind at that point, but he was certainly still alive.

The rest of the evening, the family was chilled by the cries, groans, and growls that filled the frigid night air. Regardless of his ultimate condition, Gabriel surely was in pain both physically and emotionally. He felt angry, betrayed. The sound of his hooves scraping on the wooden beams of his stall were frightening. If he escaped, they felt the hog would come for them, and take them along on his inevitable journey to the other side. "It's like he wasn't meant to die," Ruben told his mother. They only wished Roy was around.

The next day, Roy's truck rumbled into the driveway. Relieved to be home, he glanced around expecting to see the carcass hanging from a backyard tree, preliminary cuts made to drain blood. When it wasn't there, he noticed the hog was still in its stall. When he entered the home and Becca explained what had happened, Roy was furious. "Of course he didn't die!" Roy exclaimed. "His damn skull's this thick—the shot only stuns 'em. Then you run in with the pig sticker and take out his spine." Now if you don't happen to know, a pig sticker is a very long, sharp dagger, designed to pierce a hog's tough hide and destroy his vitals. So the actual killing is gruesomely hands-on. "Now the meat's gonna taste bad!" Roy said.

Without hesitation Roy went out with his .357, a more powerful round, and found Gabriel in a panic. It took a while to land the right shot, and then Roy jumped the fence and pounced on the critter like a man at war, slashing deep into the beast and ending Gabriel's life quite quickly and bloodily. He demanded his son's help at that point and the two hoisted the 350-pound (159-kg) porker onto an oak tree where his veins were dumping in no time. Roy was visibly upset as he tried to explain to his son: "I guess you hadn't listened well to me, Ruben. I told you it was important to keep him calm before he dies. You walk up real gentle, just like what you did, and nail him in the head, just like what you did. But then you gotta finish him off quick with the knife. Otherwise, once he comes back around, he's not the same. He's all riled up and scared. His heart pumps harder, filling the tissues with blood, and his adrenaline's sky high. A pig don't taste right after all that."

"How does he taste?" asked the boy.

"Like fear," Roy answered.

After a whole year of anticipation, a sense of melancholy settled over Christmas Day. The family, even Roy, missed Gabriel. The entire affair was a hard lesson in life and death. No one spoke about it much, but when the heavy packs of raw pork set on the kitchen counter, no one wanted to go near them. Finally, when Roy, enlisting Becca's help, unwrapped them to begin preparation, the wife mentally distanced herself from the task. She didn't want to think about the meat being the creature they'd owned and known for so long. No one dared criticize the situation though. Everyone knew the effort Roy had put into the feast, and he was already brooding somewhat over the mishandling of the pig's death. From time to time, he'd mumble something about the flavor, followed by "it's a shame."

Finally, as the cold winter sun began to dwindle, the family sat down for Christmas dinner. It was a beautiful spread, candlelit with holly. But the mood was not light and merry. Thick slabs of pork were pre-cut on each plate, and everyone silently watched to see who would dig into Gabriel first. Not surprisingly, it was Roy. After saying grace, he anxiously sawed off a good chunk and gobbled it down. The butcher nodded knowingly, each eye upon him. "It's still good," he said. "But you *can* taste that. It's gamey...still good, though."

Becca ate the pig next, then Ruben, then the girls. Becca agreed that the meat was good, especially with salted mashed potatoes piled on, but not another word about the pork was said. As the meal continued, and those at the table were struck by the initial sensations of being stuffed, they began to hear it. A slight, high-pitched whining outside seemed like the bitter wind. But then it changed, rose in volume, became those grunts and moans that had haunted the family when Gabriel agonized all night. Everyone looked at each other. They knew there was no other pig around, and the hair on Becca's neck stood, bristling like Gabriel's must have when he was slaughtered.

Eventually, the squealing grew too strong to be ignored. Ruben was the first to start feeling nauseated. He hid the sickness, going to the bathroom apparently to relieve himself in the usual manner. But they could soon hear the groans as he vomited in the toilet. This triggered one of the girls to feel sick, and then Becca. Each person who left the table went in a different direction to escape the miserable sounds. It was undeniable: a hog was crying in the frosty night as they tried to eat. Finally, Roy got up to look outside.

Seeing nothing through the window, Roy put on his coat. As he ventured out the door, a blast of chilly wind swept through the house. Within moments, the cry of the pig was replaced by a new sound—the scream of a human—of a man. Everyone rushed outside panting. Only 10 feet beyond the doorstep lay Roy, half-rolling on the ground, holding his leg in near-breathless pain. "Oh God!" he repeated. "Oh God!" They tried to help him up, but he refused to move. Ruben turned on the porch bulb, revealing a light dusting of sparkling snow on the ground.

"Did you slip?" asked Becca. Roy nodded in affirmation. He continued to refuse movement, and the family oriented itself so that more light would fall on his leg. They were shocked. It looked like his right leg had another joint—it was completely snapped and bent back in the middle of his shin. Upon gaining a clear view, everyone around immediately groaned in pain, barely comprehending the awful sight. Immediately, "911" was dialed.

The doctor could scarcely believe a simple fall had produced such a clean break. Needless to say, it set Roy back for a long time. Months afterward, when his sense of humor returned, he joked that it wasn't actually the fall that had gotten him. Instead, he claimed it was the jaws of an unseen creature hitting him, probably Gabriel, chomping down, breaking that shin like a corncob. And yet, oddly enough, after making the joke, Roy himself would hardly laugh. He knew that Ruben and Becca claimed they'd found circling pig prints in the snow around the house.

Whether or not it was indeed the spirit of Gabriel that had come back for revenge, or simply an imprint of his cries that prompted his killer to slip on an icy walkway, is debatable. The hog was never heard again, nor was there any sign of his ghost. But nonetheless, to whatever degree he may have returned temporarily from the other side, it made a much more substantial impact. Last I spoke to Roy, the rest of his family had not eaten a bit of meat since. And he himself has given up on raising livestock personally. Of course, he reassures me, all that could change at any time. "They just have to be hungry enough," he said.

The One That Spoke English

Few of us think of speaking to a pet verbally and actually receiving a verbal response. Of course, most people don't own a parrot—especially an African Grey. They are widely considered the cream of the bird crop. Greys might be the smartest of birds, at least those that can speak, and frequently live more than 40 years. It's no wonder that a complex relationship can, in fact must, exist between the parrot and its owner—at least to maintain a psychologically healthy pet. I was understandably fascinated by a man named Gerald who contacted me about his African Grey's spirit.

Gerald lived in New Mexico, and had a life he described as "unfulfilled" until 1981. Despite a few dates his senior year in high school, and a brief fling with a coworker a few years later, he'd found no satisfying romantic relationship. Though Gerald wanted a wife and children, he wasn't willing to settle for the types of women who wanted him. He thought of himself as a geek, extremely interested in science, especially astronomy. Because of his emotional availability, when he met an African Grey in 1979, it opened his mind to new possibilities.

The Grey Gerald first encountered was performing at a local nature center. He and a friend had gone on a weekend and were lucky enough for a bird program to be scheduled. The African Grey stole the show, and afterward he stuck around a long time, conversing with a handler about the animal. Perhaps it should be noted the handler was an extremely attractive brunette, and that may have initially sparked his interest in the subject, but after lengthy conversation, Gerald fell in love with the feathered creature, as well. He didn't take owning one seriously, however, until a couple years later when the opportunity presented itself.

Gerald perused a local pet store looking for a dog. He was, quite simply, tired of being alone, and considered an animal companion preferable to none. However, the birds caught his eye. And when a sales girl came to pitch animals, he mentioned a fascination with African Greys. "Really!" exclaimed the store employee. "A woman was in here the other day who has one to sell." For the first time, he thought of seriously owning one of the creatures. It was a sizeable monetary investment, but he'd saved quite a bit of money from his job as a teacher. Within days, Gerald was sitting in the living room of the woman, and her husband, with the Grey.

The bird's name was "Snappy." He was called that not because of a propensity to bite, but due to his wit and quick responses. Snappy was tall (about a foot) and grey (of course) with a deep maroon tail. His owner said she and her husband simply did not have the time required to keep their pet occupied, and hoped someone else could provide the love Snappy demanded. It didn't take much convincing for Gerald to whip out his wallet. Once he and the Grey exited, Gerald felt elated. An amazing animal—a talking, intelligent bird—was all his.

Right off the bat, Snappy did not like Gerald. In fact, the animal seemed to resent being sold. The bird would not acknowledge his owner to any significant degree, and only repeated generic phrases like "I'm hungry," or "what's up doc?" Gerald knew the transition would take time. And, sure enough, within months, Snappy was saying "I love you." At that point, the creature's true intellect emerged, as it would often comment on Gerald's moods. "Gerald sad?" or "Gerald happy?" were the most notable. And Snappy was quite vocal about his own moods, as well. Without getting into all the ins and outs of how amazing the creature was, Gerald told me simply "Day in and day out, year after year, he was my best friend." And then came Pamela.

Pamela was a "blonde bombshell" according to Gerald. She was a substitute teacher at his high school. They met in the break room one morning over a cup of steaming coffee and things would never be the same. He took her late one clear evening to see the Perseid meteor shower and she was hooked. As their sweeping romance grew, Gerald's hours at home slowly dwindled. And the jealousy of Snappy gradually swelled. The Grey needed stimulation from his owner, but Gerald was occupied with his newfound companion. Things didn't reach the critical point, though, until a year later.

Her entire life, Pamela had dreamed of a week in the Cayman Islands. In younger days, she was an avid snorkeler, and those Caribbean waters are some of the clearest in the world. She begged Gerald to save up time for a two-week vacation. One week would have been plenty for him, but she considered the first week as an adjustment period and second as the "real deal." The importance of this trip to Pamela was exceptionally prominent, and without much hesitation, Gerald made whatever plans were necessary to please his better half. In fact, he even thought of popping the big question on the last day.

So off they went into the great blue yonder, leaving everything else behind, including Snappy. Gerald gave the bird to his friend Tim, a chemistry teacher, for the duration. But the Gray obviously did not like what was happening. Tim was not particularly interested in the bird, and primarily kept the creature in a dark back room of his house, often under a cloth, with the door closed. It was a terrible situation for such an intelligent little being.

Among the world of African Greys, in fact parrots altogether, it's well known that such a creature can, without the proper mental stimulation, become insane. We can't be sure of what happens in the brain when this occurs, but it seems to have set in rather quickly with Snappy. In only days, he began pulling out his shiny feathers. Frequently, once this process begins, it does not end. It's too late.

When Gerald and Pamela returned from a wondrous trip to the tropical Caymans, they were engaged. Each person's mind was in a swirl of thought, absorbed with plans and visions for the future. Gerald couldn't believe his luck. But when he arrived at Tim's house to collect Snappy, he was shocked. One glance at the rattled, balding creature was enough to realize its tortured state. Only then did Gerald fully understand how delicate and sensitive the parrot's mind had been.

No words, or amount of physical contact, Gerald gave seemed to bring Snappy back. The creature was lost in its own mind, a place barely understood even by zoologists, and virtually unobtainable once the creature's grasp of our reality was gone. Seeing what had occurred, and being an animal lover, Pamela was especially distraught by the bird's condition. After consulting vets, they were able to bring the Grey back around somewhat, but he would never be quite the same. Ironically, Pamela's concern for the bird would eventually prove to be its undoing.

One weekend, while Gerald attended an educational conference, Pamela was left to care for Snappy. She took him from his cage and spent hours conversing. At one point on Friday night, Pamela decided to indulge a craving. She opened a candy bar and was surprised when Snappy said "chocolate."

"Do you like chocolate?" she asked.

"Yes," said Snappy.

After a brief deliberation, she decided to include the Grey in her pleasure. Snappy eagerly devoured the candy bar chunks, and was delighted in doing so. "Snappy happy," he'd say. Feeling guilty about the romantic trip, keeping the parrot in a good mood was her goal. And so she fed him several pieces of the rich, delicious substance. Many know that chocolate is toxic to dogs, but birds? To this day, we can't be sure. Yet, sadly, that sweetness may have been the very kisses of death. The next day, after seeming agitated, then out of energy, Snappy was dead.

When Gerald returned Sunday night, it was a morbid scene. Pamela was quite upset and in deep depression feeling she had surely done something wrong. After all, the Grey died on her watch. It only compounded her feelings of guilt. And for Gerald, the death of the bird resounded deep inside him. At a time when no one else was there, he and Snappy had shared profound experiences, that thrill which can only be gained by human-animal communication. Gerald fully realized how wondrous a creature his late pet had been, and he felt like a horrible person for allowing his dear companion—that helpless little pet in his captivity—to frazzle hideously, descend into madness, and die in irresponsible hands. It was a rough time.

Gerald spared no expense in having a fine little mahogany casket made especially for his pet. After a painful funeral in his backyard, sprinkling the ground religiously with Snappy's favorite feed, he and Pamela moved on. The incident seemed like the proper closing of a chapter, the transition from one phase of life (Gerald's existence as a single man), to his new human relationship. Snappy was dead and "that was that." There were no hints of a haunting afterward. The bird did not follow them in the house to caw and draw attention from the other side. Everything was peaceful, stale and melancholy even, for at least a week. Then the weirdness began.

One evening, as Gerald removed a soda from the fridge, he heard a high-pitched voice: "Gerald and Pam," it exclaimed. Gerald snorted, went into the living room where his fiancé was watching television, and said "What was that for?"

"What?" said Pamela, confused.

"Why did you say that?" asked Gerald.

"Say what?"

Gerald looked at her suspiciously with a slight smile on his face, but after a few moments he could tell she was seriously perplexed. "You didn't hear that?" he asked. When he explained what he'd experienced, Pamela pretty much blew it off. She was absorbed in the television program and seemed slightly annoyed to have been distracted. So Gerald dropped the issue, feeling his mind must be tricking him—making some normal sound, like an internal mechanism of the fridge, emulate the bird's voice playing on his perception. After all, he was used to hearing Snappy, and it made perfect sense for his brain to interpret a random sound as one to which he was familiar. He didn't know what the phenomenon was called, but felt assured there was a term for it in some textbook out there somewhere. But this phenomenon kicked in again the next day, this time with Pamela.

With slight reservation, Gerald said Pam was actually on the toilet when the second incident occurred. She was reading some celebrity gossip magazine when a voice said "Gerald and Pam." When she emerged from the bathroom, Pamela thought Gerald had played a video or audio tape of the bird. Gerald was excited to realize his fiancé had heard the voice, and phrase, the same as he did. He immediately realized it must be Snappy's ghost. After a short conversation, Pam agreed. The voice was too clear to be blown aside. And so then they wondered why, of all things the Grey could say, "Gerald and Pam" was what both had heard.

"Maybe it's his way of congratulating us on our love," Pam said. "Maybe he's saying he wants us to be happy without him." It sounded like a fitting explanation. Afterward, Gerald and Pam sat in the bedroom and spoke out loud to Snappy's spirit. Pam went first.

"I'm so sorry I gave you chocolate," she said. "I loved you and wanted you to be happy. I gave you chocolate because I thought you wanted it and would be happy. Please forgive me and rest in peace little Snappy. I will never forget you."

When Gerald spoke to the bird's soul, he became highly emotional, barely able to speak through tears. "You might feel betrayed," he said. "I took you at one point in my life, devoted forever, then things changed. I can only hope you're now in a better place." During the session, what can almost be called a séance, nothing paranormal occurred. The parrot's spirit seemed to be at rest. A sense of closure fell on the scene.

The next day, a Saturday, Gerald decided to do some yard work. As he trimmed hedges outside the house, the high-pitched voice came again. "Gerald and Pam. Gerald and Pam." Gerald yelled for Pam, hoping she could run into the yard and hear it, as well. When she came from the house, all was quiet.

"Listen," Gerald raised a finger to his lips.

Sure enough, in a few minutes the bird's distinct voice broke the air. "Gerald and Pam." It was the first and only time the two heard Snappy's ghost together. They walked to his grave and spoke kindly to the lost pet's spirit. Because the voice was so clear, Gerald wondered if the Grey's apparition might also appear. He stood at the burial site for a bit, then finally sat down in patience. But Snappy never appeared. Gerald had always been indifferent about an afterlife, but that day changed him.

"I really can't say whether or not Snappy was alive in some other place," he recounted. "But saying my and Pam's name together seemed like he was conscious, maybe watching us. Whatever was happening, I don't think death is the end of us."

Now that could be the ending of a beautiful story. However, life is not always so kind. Only a few days later, Gerald heard Snappy's voice again. That time he was in the shower. This was the same bathroom in which Pam had heard the bird, so we can wonder about that location's connection to the other side; maybe the amount of moisture in the air made an impact. Regardless of how and why things fell into place, as Gerald lathered his head, Snappy's voice said something unexpected. "...ick and Pam."

Gerald paused and listened again for the voice, wondering exactly what had been said. Because he wasn't expecting to hear anything in the background of the water, the whole thing threw off his perception. Though he couldn't be certain what was spoken, he knew it was something different from "Gerald and Pam."

Later the same night, as he watched television and Pamela dosed, Snappy's voice resounded clearly again. "Rick and Pam. Rick and Pam." Gerald woke up Pam so she could bear witness. But she was groggy and the voice didn't speak again.

"He said something different," Gerald noted. "I think it was 'Rick and Pam.'"

With that, Pam's eyes lit up in a shocked way. "What?"

"Rick and Pam," Gerald repeated. For the first time, he felt a bit sick.

Without going into the details of denial and deception that accompany many broken relationships, after hours of emotional wheeling and dealing, the truth was revealed. During their entire engagement, Pamela had been seeing an old high school boyfriend named Rick. There's no sense in exploring how gutted and alone Gerald felt at that point. His relationship with Pamela had been, to some degree, a farce.

I'm not certain regarding what became of Gerald's and Pamela's relationship. He didn't say and my interests were elsewhere, on Snappy's spirit. That's the interesting point. The parrot never appeared again. Whether audibly, visibly, or synchronistically, no sign was again recognized; it seemed the pet had finally passed on completely, leaving the situation behind. It's easy for us to see this tale as a marvelous fable of justice. It's one of those few genuine experiences that seem to fit a tidy storyteller's mold, complete with a twist ending. But Gerald doesn't see his experience in such lighthearted terms.

"It was the strangest period of my life," he said. "As a teacher, I'm in a position of knowledge every day to lots of young people. But it's kind of embarrassing to say I can't explain what happened there."

As is usually the case, when ghostly events are unfolding, no one realizes what's happening. But in retrospect, the collective incidents are startling. For all we know the voice of Snappy was being experienced subjectively, some outcropping of the subconscious, perhaps born of guilt. Yet that perspective would only fit Pamela because she was the only person who knew the whole truth. So we can therefore believe Gerald's own psychic potential was opened, or some other exceptional channel, manifesting by way of the parrot's voice in his mind, or we can accept a more basic premise. Snappy was an example of the most advanced animal that can speak to humans verbally. Let's take the subject at face value. Both Gerald and Pamela said they heard the parrot's voice externally. And then Snappy told Gerald something that not only changed his life, but also saved him. This is a classic theme of ghostly activity. There's no reason we should think it varies in this case just because the ghost was that of an animal. When pets can literally speak, what else should we expect?

An Entire Farm of Spirits

The Jackson Farm in Lancaster, South Carolina, may be one of the most haunted places in the world. Not only was it near the site of Buford's Massacre, which took place during the American Revolution, but an old slave church thrived there for decades. Though the structure finally crumbled away, the soil around the place is probably still packed with bodies from the graveyard—worn remains of people who lived hard, brutal lives. Layer by layer, centuries of pain and sadness drenched the secluded countryside. In the 1990s, when the Jacksons, Mark and Lynn, built their farm in the midst of it all. The paranormal events that followed shouldn't have been surprising, especially for Lynn Jackson: she was already all too familiar with spirits.

As a child growing up in Virginia, she first experienced sensitivity to the other side. By the age of only nine or 10, Lynn had cowered from human apparitions on a couple occasions. What she saw one drowsy summer evening was exceptional. Her stepfather's father had died, and the funeral was being held in a nearby state. Therefore you'd think, if a paranormal visitation occurred, it would be the dead man's phantom, drifting back one last time to comfort a mourning family. But, ironically, that was not the case at all.

Being so young, Lynn was not allowed to attend the funeral. Instead, she stayed at her grandfather's house along with her aunt's family. It was a tall, wooden home, and her bed—the living room couch—was far from the entrance. One would pass through three doors, and up a long flight of hardwood steps to reach the elevated apartment. That night, everyone was sound asleep except for Lynn. She lay alone, thinking and feeling, watching pale moonlight shine through the kitchen windows. The sight relaxed her, perhaps opened her senses. That's when she heard it first.

Though she didn't hear any of the doors open, she immediately recognized the heavy, clicking noises slowly ascending the wooden stairs. It was the sound of a creature's footsteps. The only animal in the house, a small mutt, slept closed in her grandfather's bedroom downstairs. As the steps advanced, so did Lynn's fear. The child hunkered down on the couch, unsure of whether or not to scream. It paused at the top of the steps on the opposite side of a door, the only thing separating it from the room. And then the door slowly creaked open. In terrible suspense, she held her breath.

The scream that almost came from Lynn's mouth was abruptly stunted when her throat seized in fright: a huge, black dog quietly slipped into the room and nearly seemed to glide as it came straight for Lynn. In moments it was on top of her, and the child was paralyzed, horrified that one motion would prompt the beast to attack her. It leered down with piercing, otherworldly eyes. But almost as quickly as it entered, the massive creature turned and vanished back down the stairs. Lynn was still afraid to move, and laid there in silence for many hours until the first warm rays of the sun finally shattered the eerie darkness.

Lynn discovered that all the doors had been shut and bolted. There was no explanation for the canine intruder. The incident was obviously disturbing to the child, yet the rest of the household was still more distracted by the human death. It appeared there was no connection between the funeral and her visitation. However, when Lynn later told her mother about the event, her mother's eyebrows rose. Once a large, black German Shepard lived on that property, and it had died there long before. Was it the spirit of that animal which came back, perhaps attracted by the morbid mindset of those in the house? Or was that creature an elemental black dog? We may never know, but that incident certainly foreshadowed what Lynn would experience as an adult.

Shortly after buying the property, as their farm grew, heartbreaking events started to occur. Some of the first victims were her horses. Since childhood, Lynn had dreamed of owning a pony. That dream came true when she obtained Rebel. Though it's difficult to choose a favorite from an entire farm, Rebel was paramount. He spent his days lavished with treats and all the love the Jacksons could give him. You can imagine the absolute horror when Lynn walked into her haunted barn one day to find Rebel, a completely healthy animal, lying dead and cold on the ground. And, even more shocking, Lynn's horse Ms. Kitty was lying dead next to him. Her world spun in nauseating disbelief. To this day, no one can explain how, or why, Rebel and Ms. Kitty died, especially at the same time and place. But things got even more weird.

Another of the Jacksons' beloved horses, Noah, was also in perfect health when Lynn's young daughter, Amber, noticed something strange. Noah was stumbling in the pasture, seeming dazed and distracted. Panicked with flashbacks of Rebel and Ms. Kitty, Lynn immediately called a vet and gently led Noah to the barn for rest. Familiar with the property's dark history, the female vet arrived with a Bible in hand. Her examination of Noah turned up nothing specific, and she prescribed a few basic medications. With that, the vet was shocked to see a bizarre white streak of light pass behind Lynn. Frightened by the sight, the rattled vet left in a hurry. Shortly thereafter, Noah became another casualty of the Jackson farm. He died in the exact same spot as the other two horses.

Photos courtesy of Lynn Jackson.
The peaceful Noah in life.

After many ghostly occurrences culminating with these deaths, Lynn became obsessed with gaining photographs of her property's spirits. She felt such images would add an element of proof to what she and her family were experiencing. The result is one of the most compelling collections of paranormal pictures in existence. Only days after Noah's death, she photographed the area where he was buried. The photo was stunning.

**Photo courtsey of Lynn Jackson.
Noah's apparition.**

Lynn apparently captured a picture of Noah's apparition. The profile of his body is clear, yet spectrally-nebulous. The outline of his neck and head is particularly distinct, and the entire phantom is an orangish-red, like the color of fire, as warm as Noah was in life. Though one horse looks basically like another, one can easily see the similarity between the phantasmal photo and pictures of the animal in life. And that was not the only time she seemed to capture a horse apparition.

On another occasion, she took an even more surprising picture. One might expect to photograph a ghost over its own grave, but what about a horse in your house? Lynn thinks another of her images shows Rebel in her living room! The bright outline of the pony exudes energy and motion, the rambunctious equine as full of life now as ever. Perhaps Rebel returns the love the Jackson's gave him by spending time in their domain, intimately close to them in the house, something impossible for him in physical life.

Photo courtesy of Lynn Jackson.
Could this be a horse running through the house?

In 2005, the weirdness at Jackson Farm reached a new level. Though the property had been for sale a while, no buyers had come forth. This shouldn't be surprising, given that such paranormal activity is a burden for most people, especially when animals are dropping dead mysteriously. So the place continues to function as a rescue, just as always. Even as I worked on this book, Lynn contacted me with a perplexing update. They had owned six horses for a while, but recently obtained a seventh. Because he's white, his name is Frost.

Frost was warmly welcomed to the farm. The old horse had spent most of his life working in a rugged riding camp. He'd performed nobly, always trusty and gentle, but the work was hard and demanding. When his body started breaking down from old age the camp owners knew it was time to retire one of their best steeds. The Jacksons were more than happy to have him join their family.

Photos courtsey of Lynn Jackson.
Frost lies on Noah's grave as if it were his own.

Lynn said Frost immediately reminded her of Noah. "He almost has the exact same personality," she said. "He's a very sweet, older horse." In the beginning, though Frost didn't know Lynn well, he'd still follow her around the barnyard, just like Noah. Also, when someone finished petting him, he'd use his head to softly nudge them, requesting additional petting. Noah did the same. It would break Lynn's heart to see Frost spasm a bit from abdominal distress from time to time—"colic" she called it. She would give him a pain shot and put him up to rest for the night. But only a short while after settling into the farm, the horse began doing something very strange.

Noah's gravesite is a sacred place on the Jackson farm. It's marked by a circle of stones. All of the other horses, some around for years, paid the spot no mind. However, Frost began spending a great deal of time wandering around it, staring down at the site, seeming to reflect. And then he surprised everyone by lying down on the grave as if he himself were dead, entombed within the ground below. At first, the Jacksons were alarmed, assuming the beast had a problem. But he was fine, melancholy at worst, simply resting in this odd state. To this day, he spends much of his time there, often standing there all night long! Lynn Jackson, an expert on horse behavior, is amazed. She has no ordinary explanation for why this has occurred. "Is Frost psychic?" she asked. "Is he picking up on Noah's spirit here on the farm?" Those are good questions.

I am no expert on horse behavior, but the situation immediately strikes me as possibly being of a psychic nature. Frost's kindness toward the Jacksons could be conventionally explained by his occupation for so long, meeting an array of strangers and becoming at peace with being utilized by them for recreation. But perhaps this is more than simple conditioning. Maybe the horse was so successful in getting along with humans because he could understand them on a deep, perhaps telepathic, level. Maybe he's what one might call an *empath*. These are individuals, human or animal, that are naturally sensitive to, or *empathetic with*, another creature's feelings and mindset. Because Noah's presence is apparently strong enough to not only materialize in apparitional form but also be photographed, another horse, a psychic one, would easily pick up on Noah's saddened spirit. It's bothersome to think Frost might adjust his energy so closely to the dead horse's that he expedites his own demise. Nonetheless, when Frost is lying there still, limp, and sprawled like a snowy corpse, he seems at peace. Lynn was quick to mention her steed is not a "trick horse" that has ever been trained to do that sort of thing. She also questioned whether some type of reincarnation might be occurring.

When examining tales of paranormal pets, I often hear owners speculate on the idea of the animal being a reincarnation of either a lost, beloved pet, or even a human. Generally the concept of reincarnation depends on the death of one being before the birth of the other. It's difficult to understand how a reincarnating soul could replace the one already existing in a living creature (though there are some who believe even this is possible). Personally, I don't think Frost's episode is the product of a reincarnation for that reason. And yet, to some degree, we may all be part of the same spirit anyway. Perhaps some animals are closer to each other than usual. That might be the case with Frost and Noah. How many strangers do you pass on a crowded city street? These are generally people with whom you have no history and will never see again. Yet, regardless of how different you may be from them, you and they share a powerful connection. Something brought you, and them, to that specific place, at that specific time. To that extent, you share a commonality. Whatever happened in the lives of Noah and Frost, they ended up at the same farm with the same loving caretakers. Their circumstances were similar in at least that respect alone. Maybe a spiritual connection between the equines also exists in that manner.

One of Lynn's photos of Frost at night is outstanding. Directly in front of him is a huge orb, with a smaller one seemingly behind him.

Photo courtesy of Lynn Jackson.
Frost with orbs.

What are orbs? That's a big question with many possible answers. Put simply, pictures taken at places where ghostly activity is reported often show balls or circles of light. Most so-called "orb photos" are caused by reflections, dust, moisture, and insects, but not all of them. After ruling out those things, there are some truly weird examples of unexplainable images. There seems to be some kind of association between orb-like anomalies and paranormal activity beyond our current understanding. One possible tantalizing clue as to the meaning of orbs may involve findings of the Cuza University in Romania.

In 2003, physicist Mircea Sanduloviciu and his colleagues made a startling announcement. By replicating conditions believed to exist on our infant planet, they created "blobs" of plasma that seemed to be alive. They constructed a chamber of argon gas in a plasma state then introduced powerful arcs of electricity, representing lightning storms. Cell-like spheres of plasma were spontaneously created in less than a second. The spheres had an outer layer of negatively charged ions, and an inner layer of positively charged ions, forming clear boundaries. These spheres could grow, replicate by dividing, and even "communicate." Such communication was the result of a sphere emanating electromagnetic energy, causing others nearby to vibrate at the same resonance. Sanduloviciu believes these may have been the first forms of life on our planet. "The emergence of such spheres seems likely to be a prerequisite for biochemical evolution," he said.

Could these simple, plasma life-forms be the same as orbs? Perhaps they exist due to, or are created by, the intense energy expended during paranormal manifestations. Of the many theories offered to explain orbs, this one could be the most insightful. Currently, we can't be certain of why orbs appeared in Lynn's photo. But we *can* speculate as to what all this means.

Why did the horses die? What allows them to so prominently return as apparitions? Why is the psychic connection between living and dead so strong? To answer those questions would be to address a much larger issue. The history and breadth of events at Jackson Farm are broad in scope—too broad for our current focus on the animals alone. But, sure enough, there seems to be something about the place itself that is conducive to ghostly visitors. Maybe that property is what we might call a warp: a place where the laws of physics don't always seem to apply; where frequencies can be lowered or increased due to some variables we don't fully understand, perhaps geological. Or, in other words, it could be a place where the veil between this world and the next is somehow thinned. That possibility is greatly emphasized by the most amazing creature apparitions on the Jackson property of all. They can only call them dinosaurs. Yes, *dinosaurs*.

It all began early one dark-blue evening when the Jacksons' young son, Adam, went to the barn for his chores. He watered the troughs for each animal as he'd done many times before. But that particular evening a large sense of movement caught his eye. Adam lifted his gaze from a faucet to the most incredible thing he had ever seen. Near the front of the barn a massive creature, mist and smoke churning around it, hung in the air, slowly flapping its enormous wings. Lynn recalled, "he said it had a wide wingspan and a long neck with some kind of huge bird head." The boy was absolutely frozen with fear, watching the smoke swirl up and around the beast with each beat of its wings. Finally the monster rose in the sky then vanished. Adam dashed into the house, stammering a hysterical description of what he'd seen.

 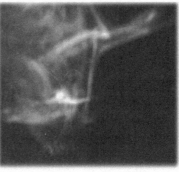

Photo courtesy of Lynn Jackson.
These misty-winged creatures may be apparitions
of prehistoric animals.

Later that night, he drew a picture. But the illustration wasn't necessary: in time, the creature was apparently photographed.

In coming years, the pterodactyl-like beast was seen repeatedly along with other visions resembling dinosaurs. Witnesses sometimes described them as huge reptiles or dragons. With time, Lynn was able to capture photographic evidence for these entities. Though misty for sure, images of the phantimals were often defined enough to certainly match the forms apparent to the naked human eye. Pictures of the "dinosaurs" are among the most fantastic Lynn Jackson has documented. They seem to demonstrate, once and for all, the extent to which her property facilitates shocking paranormal manifestations.

Dinosaur fossils have indeed been found in South Carolina. The most prominent are the *dromaesaurids* (small, fast, carnivorous lizards), *hadrosaurs* (duck-billed vegetarians weighing several tons and up to 32 feet, or 10 meters, long), *theropods* (powerful carnivores that walked upright) and infamous *velociraptors* (six-foot, or two-meter, meat eaters with devastating claws). The presence of these dinosaurs seems to ensure the company of many others, including those with wings that could, of course, virtually fly wherever they chose. If we're to look at the monstrous apparitions as imprints or entities, a historical argument could be made. However, we must examine an even larger possibility. In this case, perhaps it isn't even necessary for the creatures to have once occupied the Jackson property in a physical, living form in order to come back and haunt. Maybe the Jackson farm is a warp utilized, or at least open to, beings from hundreds of miles around.

For some reason this property may be a place where phantoms can materialize more easily. Because of this, perhaps spirits from a wide distance go there to access our realm. Or maybe imprints from extremely far in the past can still be seen—the power of weak energies being enhanced. At this point, we do not know for sure, but the eyewitness testimonies from Jackson Farm, combined with Lynn's photographs, are compelling to say the least. Without delving into cryptozoological possibilities, that property may exemplify the most extreme aspects of phantimals; it is a location where both conscious and nonconscious apparitions from yesterday and millions of years ago can manifest side by side.

In addition to these cases I've thoroughly presented, my files run over with recent reports of pet ghosts. Most of them are not as extensive as the aforementioned, though. In the majority of incidents, an animal's presence is simply glimpsed in a fleeting moment. Whether or not this is a purely psychological effect or something more, we can't say. Such reports are anecdotal, but the phenomenon is certainly real to those who have the experiences. During research for this book, I asked for experiences related to pet ghosts via my websites and radio program. The flood of responses was compelling to say the least. Most of the phantimals reported were cats.

They Visit Us Every Day

A woman from Virginia has seen her cat's spirit as a shadowy form and felt it rubbing against her leg. A woman from New Zealand was stunned by the green eyes of her dead cat glinting in a dark kitchen. A woman in North Carolina had three experiences, glimpsing the forms of three different felines and waking up when the footsteps of an invisible animal crossed her abdomen. Forrest Connor, a member of L.E.M.U.R. (League of Energy Materialization and Unexplained Phenomena Research) my paranormal research team (*www.LEMURteam.com*), had to euthanize his cat only to hear it milling around its food bowl days after. The majority of the experiences occur right after the death, within days or weeks at the most, and the apparitions are usually described as "shadowy forms." Owners consistently talk about the disembodied physical touch of the pet or hearing its meowing afterward. I don't know why cats are so prone to come back. Maybe that's one big reason those animals have been considered wicked or sacrilegious in the past, especially if one believes a soul that remains earthbound must have surely offended God.

News Radio 570 WWNC, the station that broadcasts my radio show "Speaking of Strange," also has a program hosted by Angela Moore, a well-known psychic (*www.Angela-Moore .com*). We've known each other for years, and Angela has used her skills to solve a wide variety of mysteries, including police cases. She frequently recounts her experiences with Wren, a female Chihuahua. Wren's "warehouse," the place she kept toys and chose to hide sometimes, was under Angela's bed. Only days after the dog's passing, her persistent scratching at the bedside could be felt by Angela. Upon looking down the first time, the psychic only saw Wren's hindquarters slip under the bed. "She was sort of glowing," Angela added. Of course, being "psychic" doesn't hurt one's chances of seeing paranormal sights!

Brad and Sherry Steiger are the famous authors of hundreds of books, including many related to animals, such as *Strange Powers of Pets* (Donald I. Fine, 1992). Much of their interest in the paranormal is the product of personal experiences. I asked Brad Steiger about some of them. He replied:

> *There are so many! Personal experiences with telepathic communication with pets and other animals have flourished since early childhood. In two instances—once as a child, later as an adult with a family—our dog fought back an invisible entity that from our perspective appeared to be quite nasty. When I was a small boy on the farm, I incurred the wrath of a badger that would happily have ripped me to pieces. Our old collie was trying his best to protect, but he was pretty long in the tooth. The*

three hunting hounds that materialized next may have been either Old Bill's spirit guides or my own, for they quickly treed the angry badger, then disappeared. No one in any of the nearby farms owned hounds, and they were never seen again. The wolf/canine is my principal totem.

Late at night in the ruins of Machu Picchu high in the Andes, Sherry and I had unknowingly provoked threatening entities that were really freaking out our small group of seekers. Again, seemingly from nowhere, half a dozen dogs manifested and drove back the entities. Once the ghostly beings had retreated, the dogs walked us safely back to camp over narrow mountain passages.

Steiger's encounters remind me of black dog phantimals. Fortunately, some of them appear to be helpful guides. Those with more sinister purposes usually are discussed more often, though. It seems natural for most to inherently fear a mysterious canine, especially in times past when more of them were running wild. But Steiger's thoughts demonstrate that the idea of totems might extend farther than mere symbolism. I'm also reminded of several extraordinary events during the devastating Indonesian tsunami on December 26, 2004. Numerous people were in a critical situation, sure of impending death, until an animal appeared—a python or crocodile—upon which they latched. The creatures calmly pulled them to safety then drifted away.

Occasionally, someone experiencing an isolated animal ghost remembers to take photos as Lynn Jackson did. This is rare, because all ghost manifestations are rare, but those of animals in particular. Animal ghosts usually don't persist as long as those of humans, despite some legendary phantimals like Europe's black dogs. But Debbie Orr of rural Southern Pines, North Carolina, took some digital shots a few days after a tragic death on her property. A tiny deer tried to jump her backyard fence. "It was so small it failed and instead hit it and bounced off, breaking its neck," she recalled. Her photographs revealed prominent orbs at the site. As in Lynn Jackson's photo of Frost, we can't be sure of what created the orbs in Debbie's photographs.

With such a long history of phantimals without scientifically detailed documentation, we're very lucky to live in this day and age. The technology accessible to most consumers makes it easier than ever to record such paranormal encounters. In terms of the human experience, it's obvious that observations of even ancient people are not that different from what modern humans report, despite our collective increase in knowledge and probabilities. So it's time more of us become conscious of making the effort to properly document these instances. After all, the average person's household will experience the deaths of more animals than humans. That makes them valuable for research into "afterlife effects." Even a few simple measures can make a big impact on how we perceive ghosts and ghostly phenomena. You can help the world understand this topic (perhaps the most important subject in the world) more by investing in some affordable tools and learning how to use them properly.

4 Documenting Your Pet's Spirit

I frequently receive e-mails from prospective paranormal investigators asking me how to become "certified" in the field. There is an inherent problem with that question. As Einstein said famously, "If we knew what we were doing, we wouldn't call it research." No one truly understands how ghosts manifest. We are intrigued by the subject primarily because it is mysterious, so how can we be truly "certified" to study something if we don't know what that *something* is? For that reason, I'm always suspect of people who claim to be certified ghost-hunters. I don't mean to imply they don't know what they're doing, but that the certification uses poor terminology. If they want to be certified, they should simply study the scientific method and properly evaluate instruments used to collect field data. I fear that many people who use "ghost-hunting" meters don't truly understand how the instruments function and the theories on which their construction are based. In order to effectively contribute to research, these are the things you should learn. Although understanding the scientific method through an

125

institution is fine, you can also learn it on your own. It's quite simple and logical. To make you a good investigator, let's put some of the theoretical philosophy from Chapter 2 into action.

The first step is to *observe*. It's quite humorous to hear scientists discount the reality of ghostly phenomena even though they've never initiated the first step. And you have to observe methodically, in a consistent manner, under various conditions (different times, night and day, rainy and sunny, different seasons) to have a *control*. That simply means you possess such an understanding of the usual environment that you will confidently know when something unusual happens. You could say that, in order to declare something as paranormal, you must first realize what's normal.

It's never normal for a ghost to be materializing at the same place and time, under all conditions, every day. Therefore, more than 90 percent of the time, something paranormal will not be occurring. If you aren't looking thoroughly enough, the chances of measuring the extraordinary are greatly stacked against you. So, generally, the more rare an event, the longer the amount of time it takes to construct a database of information about the event. Ghostly activity, that is prominent enough to be measured and differentiated from other more normal variables, is so rare that years of observation are necessary to make one significant breakthrough in science. Very few scientists can afford to take this time. They are understandably occupied with securing funding, and funding comes from making headway. Because it's easier to make headway on more common, predictable occurrences, they usually must pay attention to those. Always remember, science is designed to solve the easiest mysteries first, and science has not existed long enough, applied by a sufficient number of credible people, to fully grasp these events we still consider paranormal. That certainly does not mean such events do not occur, however.

The first step to documenting a spiritual presence is being a good observer, taking into consideration as many variables as possible. To be a thorough observer, the more you can observe the better—not only in terms of time, but in terms of the tools you use. Perhaps you only want to satisfy your own subjective thrill in experiencing the phantom of your deceased pet. That's fine; simply realize that employing the scientific method, with proper tools, will enhance the probability of you having those cherished subjective experiences. The technique will help you learn where and when to expect a manifestation. Document every conceivable variable within your means. The second step is being able to logically determine whether or not something that occurs is normal or paranormal. That's when Occam's Razor helps.

William of Occam was a 14th century English logician and friar. The principle, named for him, is that the simplest explanation is usually the correct one (and the second step in observing). If you eliminate unnecessary explanations, you should come closer to obtaining the truth. If there are two possible explanations for an event, one is that a ghost appeared from another dimension, and the other more common and understood, like a drafty house or natural buildup of electrostatic charge, go with the more common and solid one. That does not mean the more common explanation is correct though. In a particular, isolated instance, the more rare phenomenon may be the one in action. But the idea behind Occam's Razor is that over a period of time, due to the law of averages, it will altogether help you come closer to the comprehensive truth. It benefits the big picture you could say, and that's the view that will bring you more reliable success in the long run.

The third step is to *look for patterns and correlations.* What data seems possibly related to the outcome? If every three days a ghost appears only when the humidity is more than 60 percent, then eventually you can assume there may be a correlation between those conditions and the manifestation. We still cannot be certain of cause and effect at that point though. Did the environmental conditions allow a specter to appear, or did the specter's appearance cause the environmental conditions? That is a bigger question. If you are only interested in experiencing your pet's ghost, then your ultimate goal is to be able to predict a manifestation. Those who decide to become more in-depth scientists can proceed with ruling out the cause and effect details, but that part is not necessary at the most basic level of encountering an animal spirit.

Those three steps are the only parts of the scientific method with which the casual pet ghost researcher should be concerned. Again:

1. Be a thorough observer
2. Use Occam's Razor
3. Recognize patterns and correlations in your data

The most crucial part is the first part. As I mentioned, to be a thorough observer, it helps to have tools. Let's focus on those tools and how to use them properly. The most basic tool is, in fact, the human body. We are not separated from our environment, but intimately designed by it. The human body and perceptions are so mysterious that we can't deny a person may be able to detect energies far beyond any physical instrument we've constructed. A smell, a sound, a state of mind, anything you perceive should be a consideration in your work. The ultimate problem with using human senses as a tool, though, is the difficulty in calibrating them. Unless you design an experiment to see if something you experience directly relates to a specific, external stimuli, then it could be a hallucination, something you only experience internally. Otherwise, it can be beneficial to have more people around. If more people independently experience what you did, that adds a layer of reliability to the experience. This is not always the case, but is usually helpful—unless, of course, the amount of people seems to detract from the paranormal activity.

There are many variables to consider. A bit later, I'll give you some advice based on research I've conducted. But first, let's continue with describing the method you can apply yourself. Just because I've gotten good or bad results under certain conditions does not mean it will work the same way for you. The Earth is a big place, and I haven't been everywhere under every condition.

Tools

As I've emphasized, every tool is valuable. This is the case when investigating any paranormal phenomenon. If you have a device that can measure something, it's useful to keep around. Let's start with the simple stuff you probably already have around the house.

Cameras

The light we see is a form of electromagnetic radiation. A camera is therefore able to measure electromagnetism. Different kinds of cameras can give you different results, and even two of the same kind can give you different results based on the settings of each and the medium used. There is no certain type of camera that is necessarily better than another; it all depends on what you want to photograph. Usually, though, digital cameras are better than film units for two big reasons.

Digital cameras can give you instant feedback. This feature can be crucial when conducting an investigation. In the world of paranormal occurrences, because the manifestations are so rare and short-lived, time is of the essence. The sooner you can know that you're photographing something, the better. You don't have to wait for film to be developed, and, though a phantom kitty might pass your living room, if you only see it with the naked eye, it's easy to second-guess yourself after it's gone. Was it an optical illusion? Were you dreaming? A picture can be examined as long as you choose, though.

Also, digital cameras are sensitive to infrared light. Infrared (or IR) is electromagnetism at a lower frequency than your naked eyes can see. To my knowledge, all digital cameras can see IR light to some extent. An easy demonstration can be produced by hitting a button on a television remote control. The naked eye probably sees little or nothing, but if you observe the remote through your digital camera screen, you should see the light clearly. It's an IR beam, sometimes blinking, that is mostly used in these remote units. Because the camera is capable of seeing both what you can see and even more of what you don't, using one simply expands your chances of seeing a ghost. You may even have a digital camera with a special feature that allows you see even deeper into the IR spectrum, such as a night vision mode. Film cameras can take IR photos if you use special films and filters, but it's much more laborious, requiring more technical expertise to get results. It's like an automatic car versus a manual one. But if you're an aficionado, you can enjoy the customization available with the manual film technique.

Aside from the feedback rate and IR sensitivity, one of the key factors to spirit photography is shutter speed, regardless of whether you're using film or digital. Turn on a fan and the blades become virtually invisible, spinning around and oscillating at a rate too fast for your brain to perceive. But if you photograph them at the right shutter speed, they appear still. The invisible becomes visible, and usually the faster the shutter speed, the better. Test out your camera on a variety of settings to see what allows you to capture highly oscillating subjects best.

Digital cameras are more cost-effective than film. You can simply erase a useless shot and try again. Once you have the hardware, all imaging afterward is basically free and flexible. Video cameras are just still cameras that take 25 or 30 shots per second. This is useful because motion is captured, but they can also see the world closer to your eyes, reducing the ability to clearly freeze a high oscillation. You're better off using both a video and a still camera, shooting 3-D if you can (more reliable evidence from different perspectives). Just be sure not to contaminate one with the other, such as having a camera flash bounce off of something and cause a strange-looking effect, which can be confused with something paranormal.

If you're lucky, you'll obtain images of possible apparitions. Whether more clearly defined, misty, or orb-like, you may get one like those included in this book. Just be sure to use Occam's Razor in ruling out conventional illusions. As controls, take pictures of rain, snow, dust, insects, and such so you'll know how they look at different settings with different cameras. You can then rule out the usual stuff on your investigations. For more information on photo analysis, see *www.LEMURteam.com online.*

Though using cameras is convenient due to familiarity, it can become tiresome to shoot a gazillion pics around your house without any sense as to where to point the camera (aside from places your pet enjoyed in life). That's why other tools can help you learn where to direct your lens. Plus it's not always easy to analyze a picture, especially one that's 2-D, and draw a conclusion. Having information from other instruments to accompany your image makes a big difference.

If you decide to pursue serious imagery, and want to shoot 3-D, there are a number of ways to proceed. The simplest solution is to purchase a 3-D camera. They have two lenses, each positioned to represent the differing angles of each eye. If you get some spectral anomaly and it's shot in 3-D, you can generally rule out a reflection, piece of dust, smear on the lens, or something that's similarly mundane. The most common argument against orbs is that they're dust particles. Evidence that is 3-D can be especially helpful in judging that arena. If you have two images of the same spot, at the same time, and the orb only shows up on one side, it's probably a piece of dust. Dust particles are very small and, if close enough to show up, are only in a position to be captured by one lens. But if it's on both lenses, you can be assured the particle was not only prominent enough to be recorded on both, but also far enough from the camera to be recorded on both. In other words, if it's able to be recorded on both lenses, that means it's at least a few inches from the camera; and a tiny piece of floating debris that distance from the lenses should not show up.

If you can't acquire a 3-D camera that brings you satisfaction, just use two regular 2-D cameras side by side. Two still cameras, positioned next to each other, and fired at the same time, will give you the same result as a single 3-D camera. In fact, it should be better because a 3-D camera usually splits a single aperture between two lenses, reducing the quality of each image by half. When you can use two cameras to attain a couple of simultaneous pictures each will retain full quality.

There's also a difference between attaining a 3-D shot that's aesthetically pleasing and one that fulfills a technical purpose. If a single object is photographed at almost the same time by two separate camera operators, that process constitutes a technical 3-D image. Because the shots are not perfectly aligned, if you tried to combine them later to create a beautiful image, you may be out of luck. However, for the purpose of scientific research, such a pristine image is not required. Simply photographing an anomaly, with controlled shots, from two different angles, at roughly the same moment (a second or less apart) can provide the statistical information necessary to gauge your subject's distance from the cameras and other objects in the scene. If the subject is moving, you can also compare its position from shot to shot in order to determine the rate and conditions of motion.

Of course, if you're working with another photographer to obtain 3-D-like images for technical purposes, you want to make sure each of you understands the goal and is capable of working in unison. This usually involves some kind of verbal signal between each of you. One of the worst things you can do is both shoot at exactly the same time if you're using a flash. Doing so can cause flash cross-contamination. If your flashes fire at the same time the contamination can occur. The light from your flash can intersect with the other camera's making a bright, misty anomaly appear in each photograph. For that reason, using the two-camera 3-D technique is especially preferable with video cameras.

Strobe Lights

Just as your camera shutter speed can allow you to see more than the naked eye, a strobe light can help you see more with the naked eye. The example with spinning fan blades is easily duplicated with a strobing light source. Blades viewed with the strobe, at the right frequency, appear to stand still, turning the invisible, or at least translucent, visible. Simple strobe lights, such as those used at parties and dance clubs, should be beneficial. But the more serious researcher may want to invest in a stroboscope, a machine with a greater range of strobe rates, and more control over the adjustment.

To use them properly, you need only turn out all the lights and sit down with the strobe light pointed in the direction to be observed. If you're lucky, you may at least glimpse a moving form. I've had several people report seeing orbs with the naked eyes using this technique. Such orb-like anomalies are most often seen in stills thanks to the shutter speed: apparent evidence of how these methods allow one to peer more into the surrounding paranormal activity.

I've always felt a pair of glasses could be constructed to emulate this effect. They'd have to be light-sealed goggles, providing a truly dark chamber for the user. When turned on, a motor would speed by slits, only allowing limited flashes of light, from an illuminated location, to hit the eyes. Though I'm not certain such a setup would work, I see no immediate reason it should not. That's a project for the future, and such headgear probably already exists out there, though it may not have been applied to this kind of research at active locations. "Ghost glasses" might be a lot of fun, though.

Compasses

When ghosts manifest, they tend to accompany disturbances in the electromagnetic environment. There are lots of electronic gadgets out there to help you measure such fields. The range of *electromagnetic frequencies* (EMF) is infinite, and because we haven't yet found a particular part of the range in which disturbances always occur connected to all phantimals, you can pick and choose the kind of meter to buy if you find it necessary. You can determine the best device for your research/experimentation by frequency range and sensitivity. Do you want to pick up solar flares on the sun? Or measure an airplane flying miles overhead? Or do you only want something prominent and strong, a few feet nearby, to alert you? Those are decisions to make for yourself. As a professional, I have about 50 of all types, and there's never one meter that always does the trick in every case.

When and if you decide to purchase an EMF meter, you'll have to truly understand that specific tool by reading its customized instructions and doing as much research as possible. But the simplest thing in your kit should be a standard compass. I prefer an old-fashioned needle as opposed to one that's electronic. Keep in mind that, when EMF anomalies occur, they often make electronic devices stop working, or at least create lots of interference. If you can avoid that, you're better off. And that goes for any item I suggest, including the cameras. Weigh the pros and cons or use two kinds in observation.

EMFs are all around us, created by any electrical current. Not only are there huge ones being broadcast miles by radio stations and satellites, but tiny ones from the wiring in your walls, computers, appliances, *anything* electrical. As a control, the first thing you want to do is rule them out. It's easy to do because they stay consistent. Those fields usually don't float around the room or behave in some erratic way. They remain connected with the technology that creates or directs them. Any time you get an EMF, regardless of what detection device you're using, be cognizant of your surroundings and don't be impressed if the field is stable and predictable.

Compasses will not be affected by many of the artificial fields around you. Those forces are not strong enough to deviate the needle from the Earth's field. But when held close to parts of a television or monitor screen, heaters, circuits in walls, and so on, you'll notice the deviation. This is good if you want to focus on stronger fields, and not be potentially annoyed by little background stuff. The compass needle should always point north naturally under normal circumstances. So if the needle suddenly turns, especially spins or swings back and forth, something of a magnetic or electromagnetic sort is creating an influence. Those are the reactions for which you're looking.

As you walk around with a compass in hand, the movement of the needle can become a bit difficult to track if you're on a twisting path. That's usually the case inside a structure, of course. For that reason, to document phantimals, I suggest you merely place the compass on the ground/floor in one place at a time. There's nothing wrong with walking around first and then putting it down, but once it's stabilized on the floor you'll feel more secure in your results. You might even want to train a video camera on the compass for a while. That is, if you have the patience to potentially watch hours of a compass doing absolutely nothing! If you have numerous compasses, you can spread them around in different spots, and if a paranormal field moves through your house, its trail will be marked by a path of swinging compasses. A grouping of compasses, organized like pixels on a television screen, could give you a rough image of a transient field's course through a smaller patch of the location.

Because they're so cheap and accessible, compasses have lots of uses for the creative investigator. If, over the span of your observation, you consistently find one spot where EMFs fluctuate in some erratic fashion, that's a great place to focus your attention. Based on the experiences of researchers such as myself, you may have the highest chances of documenting your pet's spirit there. Electronic EMF devices are used in the exact same way. But if you use more than one compass or meter in a single location, be sure they are far enough apart to not interfere with each other.

These devices, whether simple or complex, can serve as your windows into the invisible realm of energy around you all the time. Even when environmental conditions are not right for a phantimal to materialize, knowing where to find its energy can show you where your artificial eyes, your cameras, should observe.

Fluorescent Lightbulbs

Upon materialization, if a phantimal's physical form is indeed comprised of plasma, a lot of electrostatic charges will be in the air. The easiest way to determine if such a buildup of charges, or ions, is occurring, is to use a fluorescent bulb. They illuminate when the gas that is trapped inside, typically a mixture of argon and mercury vapor in a partial vacuum, is subjected to charges.

In a dark room, when the air is dry, build up an electrostatic charge and see what happens to the bulb. There are numerous ways to do this. You can stroke the bulb itself with something like wool or a woman's stocking. Or you can drag your feet around on the carpet while touching one of the electrodes, if not the side of the glass. The bulb will easily illuminate. It blinks each time a discharge causes a stream of energy to flow within.

If you place the bulb on the floor of a dark room and observe, it will light up if there's an increase in charge. That type of reaction means the environment is probably prime for a manifestation. Needless to say, don't forget the bulb is there! Stepping on it could cause an implosive/explosive reaction with rather nasty results. Though you could walk around with the bulb in hand, you may not be able to tell if an illumination is caused by a patch of ions or the charge accumulated on your own body by the friction of moving.

The idea that an external apparition exists in a plasma state can be difficult to grasp. Just like liquid, solid, and gas, plasma is a state. A plasma occurs when a gas becomes ionized, or electrically charged. The electrons (negatively charged particles) in a plasma have broken away from the atoms, leaving the atoms with a positive charge. The charged atoms and electrons move freely, easily conducting electric currents.

Stars, such as our sun, are mostly plasma. Lightning is plasma, too. It happens when a storm cloud releases a massive electrical discharge, turning a column of air from a gas to a plasma. Auroras, such the Northern Lights, are the result of plasma from the solar wind, a stream of charged particles flowing out of the sun, interacting with Earth's magnetic field. There are human-made plasmas, too. Neon signs light up when the neon gas inside them becomes a plasma. Fluorescent lights also work by changing a gas to a plasma.

Auroras of the kind pictured here (commonly referred to as the northern and southern lights) are caused by cosmic rays, solar wind, and magnetospheric plasma interacting with the upper atmosphere.

Remember, plasma is a state of matter, not a type of matter. You can't say ghosts are plasmas any more than you can say people are solids. People have solid components, but so do rocks. Phantoms have a body that appears to exist in the plasma state, but there are natural plasmas that are not of a spectral nature. Those things might be associated with ghosts, though. An area with a high amount of electrical activity may have the conditions to trigger a ghost appearance.

We can't say that all such electrostatic forms, however mystical they may appear, are actually ghosts. In the laboratory, my colleagues and I have been able to easily create colorful plasmas that naturally take the shape of flying saucers. I wonder how often this phenomenon occurs in nature and is mistaken for an alien ship. On the other hand, maybe aliens construct the outer layer of their ships from plasma due to its natural propensity to take that shape and provide electrical propulsion.

Thermometers

When a phantimal is about to appear, or is in full manifestation, cold spots are often reported. These are isolated patches of air, usually no more than a few feet in diameter, that produce a chill when encountered. Often, an observer's hair is also reported to stand on end. There are a couple of theories regarding why these icy bubbles are present. Sometimes they move and other times they stay in one place. This might be due to a difference between transient entities and a stationary imprint or portal.

A cold spot might be present because, as a ghost attempts to manifest, it draws every bit of energy from the environment. This includes heat energy, leaving behind a colder area. Perhaps it can be compared to an air conditioner, a machine that is able to manipulate the amount of heat energy in a location. A second theory is that there is actually no change in the external temperature at all. The sensation of electrostatic charges passing across flesh can easily produce a sensation of chilliness, along with making the air stand on end. This is called an ion wind. Such a phenomenon would easily fit with the other electrical reports associated with the paranormal.

In order to document temperature changes objectively, it's really necessary to employ two types of devices. The most convenient is a noncontact thermometer. They provide instant feedback by detecting infrared radiation as a heat measurement. Such handheld units are usually available for $50 or less. However, they are primarily designed to register the heat of a physical surface. So if you're next to a cold spot of air in a house and aim the device, it might actually pick up the wall across from you instead of the air in between. But because we don't know the exact state of a manifested apparition, it's possible that an apparition *does* have a physical surface to some extent. In that case, it should be possible to get a reasonably accurate measurement. Also, an extreme source of temperature between you and a surface, like a candle flame, can be detected, as well. Overall, due to the difficulty in determining exactly what these instruments will measure, I suggest you also employ a second tool.

Common air temperature thermometers are easy to interpret. They are sensitive to the conditions in the 3-D space immediately around them. There is no question as to the location being measured. Therefore, they are actually the best of the two for scientific accuracy. It's funny how often the more simple, and fortunately affordable, devices can be most reliable. As with the compasses, numerous air thermometers can be scattered around a location to create a map of the temperature gradients. Such instruments may not respond as quickly as the noncontact devices, but given the pros and cons of both, you can see why I suggest employing each.

Though not directly related, I should also mention that humidity meters, barometers, and really any weather tools are also useful. Let me reiterate that all available information is essential in identifying paranormal patterns. A complete weather monitoring kit would be ideal. We don't yet know all the relevant variables, but a lower humidity is a good sign in many cases.

Audio Recorders

One of the most famous methods for gaining information from the other side involves using audio recorders. The method has become known as a way of documenting the electronic voice phenomenon, or EVP. Traditionally, audio recordings made at haunted places reveal snippets, a few seconds, of voices that cannot be explained. Usually, no such voice, or other extraordinary sound, is heard when the recording is made. Only upon playback can it be heard. Though the term "EVP" was originally applied to voices, the term has come to be used generically for any paranormal sound captured, and such recordings are now called "EVPs." This is redundant because the "phenomena" of EVP is plural, but that's how language and terminology develop sometimes.

A typical EVP seems to resonate and has an oscillation almost like it's being produced in a metallic chamber, or at least in some electronic form. I have heard some that do not contain those earmarks, but instead sound like a regular noise from a conventional source. I have a personal hypothesis that might explain the difference.

The EVPs with a metallic resonance are often interpreted as being an interactive voice, such as "Who are you?" I even have one from a researcher whose name is called, obviously indicating an interaction. So those types may be from entities either adjusting their energy frequencies, or in fact using another electronic device, a "telephone from the other side," if you will, to communicate. But EVPs without that sound of oscillation are not commonly interactive. I have one from a haunted house that says "Please stop!" Supposedly, a woman was abused in that building for many years. This could be a painful imprint from those times.

In either case, there is one outstanding problem with analyzing EVPs. Very rarely are the words spoken clearly enough to be immediately interpreted. That is to say, 10 people could separately be chosen to listen to the same recording for the first time, and each independently come up with a different interpretation of what's said. For that reason, most of them have very little scientific importance. However, if effective, this can be extremely useful for gaining information. As opposed to struggling over optical anomalies and erratic meter readings, it might provide a way to gain more tangible messages from another realm. So how might this work?

If you take a radio with a headphone jack, tuned to a station, and plug a large coil of wire into the jack, you will hear nothing. No air is being resonated, so there's no reason your ears should pick up anything because they require physical vibrations. Instead, the signal is being broadcast electrically from the coil, just like the programming broadcast from a radio or television tower. Turn up the volume all the way. This still doesn't matter in terms of your ears, because it only increases the voltage beaming from the wire, making no direct impact on your ears. You can even hold your head right up to the coil, but you'll hear nothing. The speakers are completely bypassed.

Next, take an audio recorder with an external microphone. It doesn't matter if you're recording on a tape or digital medium. Hold the microphone up to the coil and record the silence for a bit. When you rewind and play back your recording, you should hear whatever was on your radio loud and clear. Even though your ears heard only silence, definite audio was being passed onto your device. This demonstrates how it's possible for a sound that does not resonate air, and is therefore not audible to naked ears, to still be recorded in an objective medium. The most important aspect seems to be the kind of microphone used. Different microphones are sensitive to different ranges of electromagnetic frequencies. You could actually use an internal microphone built into some devices, but external ones seem to operate better. Using a setup like this, you can determine what microphones may be best for capturing EVPs. Just test out different ones to see what captures the audio effectively.

Because we know ghostly manifestations occur with electromagnetic disturbances, maybe they are able to be captured just like the coil's broadcast. But, in my experience, EVPs of phantimals are rare. This makes the pursuit of such results even more highly prized. To see if you can capture your pet's sounds, the process is quite simple. Just leave the device in record mode at the place you think is most likely for a phantimal manifestation. This may not necessarily be where the creature died, but an area he or she frequented in life.

The longer you let your equipment roll, the higher your chances of documenting something. When you play back the recording, listen carefully. Even something that may sound like an unrecognizable blip can be amazing when played at different speeds. Aside from features built into the recording device, there are numerous simple, affordable software programs that allow you to change the playback speed of any audio recording when input. Though you don't want to manipulate the audio too much, or it loses integrity, altering playback speed is completely understandable. After all, you must keep in mind that time is a flexible thing. Time for them may not pass at the same rate as it does for us.

Electrostatic Generators

The most unusual devices one can employ to research ghosts are electrostatic generators. These are machines that stir up the electrical environment, perhaps creating loose charges, or building blocks, that can either allow an apparition to materialize or reveal it by sticking to its form. Using such instruments to enhance ghostly activity is based on my personal research—I know of no other researchers who have proposed this before me.

Every object around you, including the air between you and this book, has a fairly balanced settlement of positive and negative charges stuck together. When you run an electrostatic generator, it starts ripping those bonds apart in the nearby environment. The result is a cloud of charged particles, blown into the air, instantly seeking out anything that will balance them. If an apparition is nearby, we can hope some of those charges will latch onto the specter, greatly enhancing its luminous visibility.

Even when a ghost is not present, free-floating ions luminesce as an enchanting blue. They snap out like miniature lightning bolts, branching in all directions. Utilizing a device that elevates this mechanism can be beneficial. The downside is attempting to operate them alongside other instrumentation with which they will interfere (and can even destroy by burning out delicate circuits).

The simplest type of electrostatic generator to have on the scene is a Van de Graaff. Most people have seen them in school. They are silver spheroids atop a tall, plastic neck with a plastic base. Within the contraption, a rubber-like belt spins on a couple pulleys made of different materials. This causes a charge to build on the belt, and although some ions are drained off by a metal jack on the base, others accumulate around the spheroid. You can place your hands on the metal spheroid to make your hair stand on end. And, in that position, a person can usually move small objects, such as cigarettes or ping-pong balls, without touching them, only holding a hand nearby, and even create levitations.

The easiest way to accomplish levitations is by incorporating two tin pie plates and a small (less than a half-inch, or a centimeter, long) piece of aluminum foil shaped like an arrowhead. Put one plate on a flat, nonconductive surface, and suspend the other a few inches above, parallel, using a piece of thread. The two plates should not touch, of course. Then put the foil "arrow" between them. The tiny piece of foil will float when you bring your electrified hand near one of the plates. At first it may be a bit tricky, finding the right balance and distance to prevent your arrow from sticking to one plate or another. But when the right variables are achieved, usually after a few minutes of adjustment, a simple levitation will occur.

By creating a levitation effect, and telekinesis-type connections to objects, you will be able to produce the kinds of reactions frequently reported when ghostly activity occurs. When that electrification occurs in the open environment, it can enhance phantasmal phenomena. Therefore, allowing an electrostatic generator to run at a hot spot, where the highest chances of a materialization are present, could magnify the environment necessary for a ghost to present itself. So, if you have a Van de Graaff, or similar machine, let it operate unimpeded. Placing something pointed, such as a metal needle, at the spot of discharge can help even more. Sharp points especially conduct charges, pouring them into the environment more rapidly. In a nutshell, you may be able to help a phantimal manifest.

Affecting Your Chances
of an Encounter

Even though the conditions to be altered can vary greatly from situation to situation, in my own experience, there are a couple things you can do to either enhance the chances of experiencing a phantimal or, inversely, decrease the chances. Not only have I had success with these methods, but I receive plenty of feedback from others for whom they have worked, as well. They are certainly worth a try on your end.

Because the manifestation of an apparition seems to depend somewhat on the buildup of electrostatic charges, the less humidity around, the better. This does not mean that a specter can't appear when the amount of moisture in the air is high. It simply means that it's easier when the humidity is low. The greater the amount of moisture, the more powerful, or energetic, the figure must be. So the simplest way to enhance your chances of an external materialization is to run a dehumidifier. This will remove water from the air and help create those conditions when you can drag your socks across carpet to get a doorknob shock.

On the other hand, running a humidifier will have the opposite effect. If you want to stop ghostly activity, the more moisture in the air, the better. I once witnessed a swirling mist in an attic during hot and rather humid conditions. Though that form was associated with a human wraith, as opposed to a phantimal, it still goes to show that a manifestation can occur when the humidity is high. But it seems the higher the humidity, the stronger (or more connected to this dimension) the specter needs to be in order to manifest.

Oddly enough, mirrors in a house can make an impact, as well. On many occasions, I've examined a haunted house to find a room where at least two mirrors are facing each other. We don't really know what impact this has on the paranormal, but after the angles are adjusted so that they do not reflect each other, creating an "infinite tunnel of images," the ghostly encounters stop. Because mirrors reflect light, a form of electromagnetic energy, they may alter the overall environment in a way that changes the conditions necessary for the phantasmal. At this point the issue is still mysterious. However, mirrors, or at least reflective surfaces, have been associated with this sort of thing for thousands of years.

The ancient Greeks made use of mirror-like communications via what they called oracles, now known as *psychomanteums*. They apparently constructed large, winding, underground labyrinths. A person mourning over the loss of a loved one would enter the dark chamber alone. This was sometimes done after weeks of the person staying in seclusion, surrounded by personal articles of the deceased in question. That atmosphere helped to focus the subject's mindset on the person to be contacted. When the time was right, the subject would traverse the labyrinth alone. At the end would be a highly-polished metal cauldron filled with water, creating a mirror-like surface. After a while of gazing into the cauldron, the dead person's face would appear in the water, eventually rising and extending from the cauldron, interacting in a fully realistic and tangible manner. Such systems of water gazing have also been used by prophets to fortell the future, known as scrying.

A modernized version of the psychomanteum is much simpler. You can set aside a room in your house that contains a chair and mirror on the wall. This mirror should be in front of the chair, but elevated slightly above eye level, so that the person seated cannot see his or her own reflection. Lighting should be low, and something to provide white, relaxing noise, such as a fan, can be added. By sitting in the dim room alone, gazing at the mirror, a state of slight sensory deprivation is achieved. Usually, after only a few moments, strange effects can be observed. The room seems to darken even more, a blackness closing in from all sides. Amorphous light forms might appear, moving around in an abstract manner. And, eventually, the same effect as the Greeks achieved will occur. A vision of the dead will appear and interact.

This kind of experience seems to be entirely subjective because it's based on placing the observer's mind in a weird state. Having been in a psychomanteum myself, one constructed by L.E.M.U.R.'s Brian Irish, I have certainly seen the aforementioned optical effects created. But I've never entered that state with the intention of contacting a specific dead person. Clearly, that mindset must be in place to make contact with a particular spirit. Regardless, the experience is obvious to everyone I know who has been inside the psychomanteum.

More detailed experimentation with psychomanteums has been done by researchers such as Dr. Raymond Moody, Dianne Arcangel, and members of the Rhine Research Center, famed extension of the late Dr. J.B. Rhine's work at Duke University in North Carolina. At a paranormal conference I produced years ago, I planned to set up a psychomanteum for random use by the guests. Researchers from the Rhine were presenting, and they were shocked, strongly deterring me from doing so, saying some people, mentally unprepared for the situation, could have a psychotic break from reality. On their clinical advice, I scrapped the idea. Therefore, I DO NOT advise that you attempt this method of contact without consulting with a physician first. And I've never heard of this being used to contact a pet, only humans. Whatever the case, that may explain why mirrors can contribute to the success, or failure, of breaching the gap between this world and that of the deceased.

Resources

This basic information in this chapter is sufficient for attempting to gain evidence of a phantimal at the most elementary level. I discuss this equipment, and more, in my book *How to Hunt Ghosts* (Touchstone Books, 2003). If you require additional information, I suggest you consult that book, as it is overall more relevant to this aspect of scientific research. You will find more information about obtaining and utilizing equipment both through that book and by visiting *www.HowToHuntGhosts.com* and *www.LEMURteam.com* online. For the most part, I see very little difference between pursuing the spirits of people and animals. In either case, you should focus on the behavioral characteristics of your subject, then adjust the investigative technologies accordingly. The most outstanding point is adjusting for height. Most animals are found only lower toward the ground, whereas most humans rise to a greater height. Imagine the position a subject occupied in physical life, and look there.

Whereas an interactive entity may be able to occupy virtually any position, and any form, imprints are quite different. I frequently hear reports from people who have seen ghosts and not realized what was being observed at first. In some cases, phantoms look so solid and tangible that they appear just like living individuals. Then the observer realizes the floor level comes up to the figure's ankles, shins, or knees. This implies the specter resides at some previous floor level from the past. An imprint still occupies the same section of space it occupied in former times. That's why people who live in brand new houses are often confused by having a ghost. "I just built this house, so how can it be haunted?" they ask. It's not necessarily about the structure, you see, but about the location.

Documenting your pet's spirit by using these techniques may seem comforting at first, but I must caution you: Many people do not accept the reality of spirits until tangible evidence is captured objectively. Then, once this coveted evidence is obtained, its implications strike an unexpected chord. Once you fully understand that spirits can exist around us, that realization may be unsettling. It compromises one's sense of privacy in the most intimate way. The idea that you may not be alone, even when you want to be, can be overwhelming, especially to children who are already struggling with a model of reality based on the world they readily experience.

After enough work is invested on the part of people like you, I predict that mainstream science will one day acknowledge the reality of life-forms nonphysical to us. At that point, a drastic change in worldviews will occur, altering civilization itself. That is, unless public denial is so great that most people simply won't accept the fact. Look at time travel, for instance. The flexibility of time has been thoroughly proven, and yet the concept is so foreign to most people that, unless they start seeing commercials about it on television, they simply won't believe it, just as the Wright brothers' flying machine or Edison's phonograph were originally called frauds. The human mind demands constant reinforcement on a personal level. It is so difficult to simply survive in this world by the most pragmatic means, most people are understandably distracted by those primitive issues alone. But the body of evidence people of the future will collectively gather should finally reach a critical point at which all that changes; ideas of science and faith can ultimately merge in the minds of most humans, altering our entire appreciation of what it means to live and die. Until we grasp that on the most basic level (applicable to everyone) such knowledge will only be used by the elite, like secrets in a government, shielding everyone from reaping its full emotional and intellectual benefits. For a while, this evidence will not sink in—it will frighten or confuse, and naturally be met with ridicule. But in the long run, your research can truly help us evolve. Here's the great irony: Our technology was invented by our spirits, yet it will take a while for our technology to prove our spirits exist.

5 Bigfoot and Loch Ness and Mothman, Oh My!

Throughout this book, we've focused on animals we all know exist. There are examples of such creatures found, living or dead, in zoos and/or museums around the world. But there was a time when many of those animals were not thought to exist. Before I delve into examples, think about how many individual creatures out there do not know *humans* exist. Even if we look at the waters alone, it's amazing to consider we've been to the moon, around 250,000 (400,000 km) miles away, but have scarcely scratched the bottom of the oceans, the Mariana Trench, only seven miles (11 km) deep at the most. That's a bit more than 10,000 feet (3,000 m) deeper than Mount Everest's height.

Modern technology gives us a false impression of the Earth's magnitude. Because we're able to see the entire blue sphere from a satellite, because mapping is so superior, because travel is so convenient, and because television can reach a correspondent anywhere in the world almost instantly, it makes Earth seem small. But in fact, there is still much land even in well-populated countries that has not been explored. Thousands of new species are discovered each year. Though most of them are tiny, such as insects, big ones are indeed found, as well.

Though reported for hundreds of years, and often thought of as a mythical sea monster, the first footage of a live giant squid (*Architeuthus*) was shot near Japan in September of 2005. Earlier that year, in May, a new primate was discovered in Tanzania. The highland mangabey, as it's called, is a substantial monkey, standing up to 3 feet (0.9 m) tall. Just a month before, the ivory-billed woodpecker was rediscovered in a remote Arkansas bayou. Scientists believed that particular species of bird had been extinct for decades.

History has given us a constant flow of new animals. One classic example is the coelacanth, a type of fish believed to be extinct for 65 million years, until one was caught in 1938 near South Africa. Now several populations are known to exist. The 10-foot (3-m) long, 300-pound (136-kg), man-eating Komodo dragon wasn't known to science until 1912, its existence disputed for years. In 1902, the mountain gorilla was discovered in the Virunga Mountains near Uganda. These enormous beasts can stand up to 6 feet (1.8 m) tall. Giant pandas were discovered in 1869 and are still some of the most endangered in the world. In these cases, I only use terms such as "discovered" half-heartedly. It's an arrogant notion because it often means "accepted by the west." In fact, most such creatures have been widely known by nearby cultures, even for thousands of years. But egocentric scientists dismissed them as products of myth or fantasy until they, themselves, obtained satisfying evidence, usually by means of a dead specimen.

An animal that has not yet been accepted by mainstream scientists, yet was reported by eyewitnesses, is called a cryptid. The study of these hidden or mysterious creatures is called *cryptozoology.* Though, in the purest sense, a cryptid is an animal that may possibly exist but has not yet been officially discovered, the term is also loosely applied to known animals that seem to appear out of place or time. For example, on October 9, 1981, in my hometown of Asheville, North Carolina, a kangaroo appeared hopping around streets near the famous, opulent Biltmore Estate. The world's top cryptozoologist, Loren Coleman, documented the event in his book, *Mysterious America.* Police and reporters gave chase, and the desk clerk of a nearby hotel exclaimed "I was afraid someone might shoot it!" But the kangaroo simply vanished, never to be seen again. There is no recorded origin for the incident, such as the creature having been an escaped pet or zoo animal. As you probably know, kangaroos aren't native to the Blue Ridge Mountains! But in 2005, similar incidents occurred in West Virginia, only a couple states north, according to the *Charleston Gazette.*

Starting shortly after Christmas 2004, a small kangaroo, or wallaby, was seen hopping around Jackson County for several months, prompting numerous calls from concerned locals. State conservation officer Clyde Armstead commented "People will call in say 'I swear I'm not drunk or on drugs, but I just saw a kangaroo.'" Finally, in mid-June, two sheriff's deputies and a state trooper cornered the creature in a partially fenced parking lot. Though they were able to photograph the 3-foot (0.9-m) marsupial, it easily escaped, disappearing into the night. As with the Asheville case, no zoos or exotic pet owners claimed the creature. "I've been a conservation officer for 17 years and have never seen anything like this," Armstead said. He told me personally he felt there was a "family" of them in the area. Upon my last contact, more than a year after the first sightings, the animal, or animals, were still on the loose in Jackson County. Of course, that county is adjacent to Mason County, where the infamous Mothman encounters occurred.

Mothman

In November of 1966, one of history's most bizarre series of events took place, and there are understandably debates regarding specific descriptions and events. It started when five gravediggers near Clendin, West Virgina, observed a large, dark humanoid form rise from a tree and fly over their heads. But you might say a couple days later, on November 15, is when the popularized era of sightings truly began. Loren Coleman's *Mothman and Other Curious Encounters* is one of the best books on the chain of events.

Two couples were joyriding in a '57 Chevy through a remote area, near Point Pleasant, where an abandoned World War II explosives (TNT) dump was located. The area was popular as a "lovers' lane." When they noticed a tall, black figure near the side of the road, they were instantly perplexed. But then its blood-red eyes glinted in the shadows, sending a chill down their spines. Instantly terrified, sensing this being was unnatural, the Chevy tore away. Then a truly startling sight: as they got a better look at the creature, demonic wings sprung from its back. "It was shaped like a man, but bigger," witness Roger Scarberry later recounted. "Maybe 6 1/2 or 7 feet tall." (That's about 2 meters tall.)

The figure clumsily moved toward the vehicle and then took to the air, chasing the horrified couples. "We were driving 100 miles per hour," (or 160 km/h), Scarberry described, "and that bird kept right up with us. It wasn't even flapping its wings." The creature stayed with them for miles, emitting a high-pitched screeching noise all the while. Eventually, much to their relief, he dropped away into the blackness of night.

That incident was reported to law enforcement, and when the sensational story hit the newspapers, an Ohio editor, a fan of the Batman television show, dubbed the creature "Mothman." This may be partly because the young couples described the creature as having no clearly defined head protruding above its broad shoulders. This reduced the being's overall appearance to a less distinct humanoid shape and more insectoid one.

Over the next year, Mothman hysteria swept the region. There were dozens of outstanding sightings, involving at least 100 people, prompting investigators like John Keel to spend time there becoming intimately familiar with the people, places, and events. He eventually chronicled his experiences in a classic book, *The Mothman Prophecies*, which was made into an eerie film with Richard Gere and Laura Linney in 2002. During this time, reports of UFOs, men in black, poltergeists and other paranormal reports also accumulated. Those may or may not have been related to the creature sightings—they may simply be the product of overactive imaginations at a time when so much emphasis on the spooky creature activity was being publicized.

Whatever the case, reports of Mothman often included a variety of bizarre characteristics. Aside from him flying without flapping his wings, others said he could lift off from the ground straight up, like a helicopter. Some described eye and skin irritation, perhaps similar to radiation burns from enhanced UV. And, of course, we have Mothman's glowing eyes. We can't be sure whether or not they produced light or simply reflected it like a cat's. Regardless, he was attributed with many qualities that are not found in any normal, physical, biological specimen known on this planet.

Photos courtesy of JoshuaPWarren.com.
The Mothman statue in Point Pleasant, West Virginia.

The usual climax of the story is that on December 15, 1967, during 5 p.m. rush-hour traffic, the Silver Bridge collapsed. Its 700-foot (213-m) span joined Point Pleasant to Ohio, crossing the Ohio River. The dark, frigid waters were filled with screaming people and Christmas gifts, a truly unsettling sight. Forty-six people drowned. The Mothman activity basically stopped afterward, many considering the entire affair to have been a chilling omen of the tragic disaster.

In the movie, there is one scene I particularly enjoyed. Richard Gere's character, John Klein, hunts down a paranormal expert named Alexander Leek ("Leek" is "Keel" spelled backwards) for insight on the Point Pleasant incidents. Klein asks why he has gained the attention of the Mothman (or mothmen). Leek replies, "You noticed them, and they noticed that you noticed them." We can't help but wonder if such a simple statement explains much in terms of our encounters with the unknown. Are our sensitivities, brought on by personal tragedies or other variables, triggering additional meetings, or at least our awareness of them?

Some cryptozoologists, such as Mark A. Hall, believe Mothman was nothing more than a huge owl. Hall coined the term "Bighoot." He explains that such a large creature could glide behind vehicles, utilizing the wind shear to save energy in flight. That would negate its need to flap wings, and the large, glassy eyes would be a startling feature. Loren Coleman points out that sightings of huge, winged creatures have a long history in West Virginia. In *Haunted Valley and More Folk Tales*, author James Gay Jones notes that such birdmen were reported in the Point Pleasant area in the early 1900s. Has that region been home to an isolated population of giant owls, or something like the Native American thunderbirds, for a long time? Was one making the rounds in the 1960s, scaring the bejeezus out of everyone, distorting their perceptions slightly? That may be the case. But, if any of the apparent paranormal qualities attributed to Mothman were real, then the creature most likely transcends our understanding of how purely physical organisms function. Perhaps Mothman was a kind of phantimal.

Maybe Mothman was the ghost of a large, mysterious owl that once lived in the area, similar to what Mark A. Hall describes. Perhaps he was the spirit of a raven thunderbird. What if that area of West Virginia is an ancient warp? Once in a while, the warp is active when some kind of misunderstood environmental change is building. During this state, it's easier for phantoms, such as the Mothman entity and others, to merge with our physical realm on a limited, temporary basis. Then, when the warp discharges, like a huge electrical capacitor, in this case causing a mechanical stress capable of breaking the Silver Bridge, all falls back into place for a while, until the next buildup occurs. Therefore, those paranormal phenomena would be omens, especially in retrospect, but not necessarily the cause of that ultimate, tragic event. Could this warp location also explain the mysterious kangaroos hopping around the countryside without explanation, eluding numerous attempts at capture, even to this day? As you can see, it all becomes quite a complicated situation, considering so many variables.

The idea of a figure such as Mothman being the ghost of a cryptid seems a bit unsettling to Loren Coleman. I asked him what guidelines should be used to separate organic creatures, existing via familiar biological properties, from phantasms. He replied, "I am interested in biology, zoology, and cryptozoology, as the basis of my explorations. If there appears to be a tangible foundation for the animal reports I am investigating, I am interested. I am interested in tangible intangibles, but not in following a path that attempts to explain one unknown with another. I find this an intellectual exercise worthy of the time of others I respect, but of no interest to me."

I asked Coleman if he feels some animals may exist in a realm/dimension that have never been physical to humans. He said simply, "I choose to not explore this question because of my [previous] answer."

I posed this same question to best-selling author Brad Steiger. Many of his books, such as *Mysteries of Time and Space* (Whitford Press, 1989), explore the cosmic boundaries of overlapping realities. He replied:

> *We and our animal companions are all multidimensional beings. If the question is how we can distinguish between biological and phantasmological beings, there are the same distinctions that we find with all so-called ghosts. Sometimes, though, we can be fooled or tricked. We have numerous accounts of people being led to safety by angelic or spirit animals—usually dogs, but in one case a deer, another a shark. I do most certainly believe that there is an unseen world that coexists with our own; perhaps several dimensions of unseen worlds. I believe that there are both benevolent and malevolent intelligences in these dimensions that can appear briefly in our physical dimension in whatever forms they choose. In some cases, these choices might involve the appearance of animals.*

From a strict cryptozoological perspective, it seems that either Mothman had to be a traditional biological organism, or was not sufficient for serious research. Of course, if in fact the creature was *not* physical in the traditional sense, such as a collective hallucination, the cryptozoologists can always speculate that he may have been, but we'll never know.

If Mothman were indeed the spirit of a great owl, then he qualifies beautifully as an impressive phantimal. But then we're forced to ask the question, if he's not the product of a bird or bat, something different altogether, is that an animal at all? What is an animal? For the purposes of this chapter, an animal shall be anything that is *not* human. And I suppose that should be our definition of an animal altogether for this book. That's for sake of convenience, because humans are technically animals, too.

The Thunderbird Photo

I couldn't get through this section of the book without resurrecting one of the most fascinating phenomena in the course of recorded history. It's an episode known as the Thunderbird photo mystery. Though I've already mentioned thunderbirds a couple times, if you don't know for sure, they're basically HUGE birds recorded by Native Americans for hundreds or thousands of years. Exactly how big? No one can say for certain, but definitely big enough to pick up a human child and carry him or her away. Even in recent times, these creatures have made the news.

In October of 2002, Alaskan pilot John Bouker, and his passengers, saw a creature outside his plane that thoroughly shocked them. A "bird" with a wingspan that matched his Cessna 207, about 14 feet (4.3 m), glided alongside the craft. Bouker told the *Anchorage Daily News*, "At first, I thought it was one of those old-time Otter planes. He's huge. He's really, really big. You wouldn't want to have your children out." As a general example, the monster was compared to something from the Spielberg movie *Jurassic Park.* According to CNN, another local pilot had recently seen the bird about 1000 feet (305 m) outside his airplane.

But the most amazing "thunderbird" incident occurred in 1890 near the notorious Tombstone, Arizona. The local newspaper, the *Tombstone Epitaph*, supposedly printed a story on April 26, 1890 about several locals who had shot and killed one of these magnificent animals, along with a photograph. According to legend, the photo showed at least a half dozen men posed beside the beast which was nailed to a wall. The bird was mentioned by writer Horace Bell in the 1930 book *On the Old West Coast.* Yet for the most part, this incident did not enter the popular consciousness until 1963. That year, a man named Jack Pearl wrote of seeing the picture in Saga magazine, a pulp publication geared toward men. Later, in September of 1963, H.M. Cranmer wrote of seeing the photograph in *Fate* magazine. However, no one could produce the actual image.

Stories regarding the thunderbird photo were fairly consistent. A group of rugged old-timers stood next to a dead, winged beast that was spread on a boarded wall. But aside from that, descriptions varied. Some claimed the wingspan was 20 feet (6 m), while others said it was more than 100. All the while, staff of the *Tombstone Epitaph* looked through their files to no avail. They claimed there was no trace of this image. Various historians poured over *Epitaph* issues without success, even as others said it had been reprinted in a variety of modern periodicals. But that only reinforced the zeal of those who claimed to have seen the picture. More and more came forth each day.

Even Ivan T. Sanderson, the famed writer and researcher of natural anomalies, claimed to have a copy of the elusive photo. Canadian researcher W. Ritchie Benedict had a particularly titillating tale. In 1971, he claimed to have watched an episode of the Canadian *Pierre Berton* talk show. On the program, Berton's guest, Sanderson, displayed a copy of the thunderbird photo on a placard. In order to find that episode, Benedict contacted the Screen Gems organization in Ontario. They were unable to produce the image, but Benedict finally received a letter from Berton, himself. In the letter, Berton said he remembered that episode, as well as the picture, but did not have a copy. Next, Benedict turned to the National Archives. They replied saying they had 67 of the shows on file—all except the relevant one.

Even John Keel, of Mothman fame, said he'd seen, and perhaps once owned a copy of the picture. According to some sources, like researcher Troy Taylor, Keel remarked "I know I saw it! And not only that, I compared notes with a lot of other people who saw it." Peter Johnson, a correspondent of the late Mark Chorvinsky's *Strange Magazine*, also said he'd seen it:

> *What I saw, in one of these magazines, and I'll never forget it, because it amazed me at the time*

because I did not think that cowboys were ever clean-shaven: And the men that are standing in the foreground there, in front of the barn, or the side of a railway car, or the side of this big house, or whatever this big boarded thing—though I seem to recall doors there, like barn doors—they had beards and broad brimmed hats like sombreros, and it was very, very unusual. I thought, how weird, cowboys never looked like that. So I've always remembered them as being miners. Whether this is true or not, I don't know.

Mark Chorvinsky went on the hunt to the best of his ability:

Peter Johnson jogged W. Ritchie Benedict's memory: he recalled he may have seen the photograph in Saga magazine, perhaps from the mid-1960s. But I went to the Library of Congress and checked out all the issues of Saga from 1958 through 1970 and I can say with all assurance that it's not in any of those issues.

To this day, no one has been able to produce the thunderbird photo. In some descriptions, it looks like a big, feathered bird, but in others it seems to have more characteristics of a pterodactyl-type creature with a pointed head and the face of an alligator. *Parascope.com* says one account describes "The beast was said to have no feathers, but a smooth skin and wingflaps 'composed of a thick and nearly transparent membrane...easily penetrated by a bullet.'"

In the mammoth Reader's Digest Mysteries of the Unexplained, a story is recounted about a pterodactyl seen alive in France, in 1856. Workers were toiling on a railway tunnel between the St. Dizier and Nancy lines:

> In the half-light of the tunnel, something monstrous stumbled toward them out of a great boulder of Jurassic limestone they had just split open. It fluttered its wings, croaked, and died at their feet.
>
> The creature, whose wingspan was 10 feet 7 inches [3.2 m], had four legs joined by a membrane, like a bat. What should have been feet were long talons, and the mouth was arrayed with sharp teeth. The skin was like black leather, thick and oily.

A paleontology student at the nearby township of Gray immediately identified the animal as a pterodactyl. The limestone within which the creature was imprisoned seemed consistent with the period in which those winged creatures lived. And the particular section of stone contained a cavity with the exact shape of the beast, forming a mold of its body. That story is credited to The Illustrated London News, February 9, 1856, page 166. Astoundingly, there is no mention of what happened to that animal, and its whereabouts are still completely lost to history. Why is this?

So was the creature in the photograph a thunderbird or prehistoric creature? And did it even exist at all? If we're to believe the reports from research authorities like Ivan T. Sanderson and John Keel, we must accept such an image does, and has been around for more than 100 years. Hence, the deepest question is why no one can locate this image.

Some researchers think the photograph cannot be located for a rather simple reason. They surmise it has never actually existed, but naturally fits into the human psyche. The idea is that the concept of some images is so familiar it neatly occupies a place in the human mind. Composites of many pictures through the years, here and there, along with bits and pieces of stories, all clump together into one representative image. And given the collective suggestion of others who say the picture exists, a recollection of this non-existent photograph is only reinforced, snowballing into a phenomenon of tangible memory that has arisen from an intangible and nonexistent source. Is this a valid possibility? Indeed, I think it is. But let's look at the alternative.

Shall we, however long the limb we must navigate, give proper respect to those devoted researchers who claim to have seen this image? Can we accept them at their words, as opposed to demeaning their thoughts and expertise? Let's say this image does exist, or at least *did* exist. What happened to it and why? Could there be a principle of reality at work so far beyond what we normally consider believable that we can't grasp what's happened here? Maybe there are multiple dimensions orchestrated by some higher intelligence that dictates the information we receive and when we receive it. It is conspiratorial to ponder this possibility, yet we shall.

Throughout journalism, we're overwhelmed with tales of amazing finds that somehow disappear from the record. I am immediately reminded of the strange skeletons discovered in the 1880s, also included in *Reader's Digest Mysteries of the Unexplained*:

Human skulls with horns were found in a burial mound at Sayre, Bradford County, Pennsylvania, in the 1880s. Except for the horny projections some two inches [5 cm] above the eyebrows, the men to whom these skeletons belonged were anatomically normal, though at 7 feet tall [2.1 m], well above the average height. It was estimated that they were buried about A.D. 1200.

That discovery was made by a Pennsylvania state historian, a dignitary of the Presbyterian Church (Dr. G.P. Donehoo), and two professors (A.B. Skinner of the American Investigating Museum and W.K. Morehead of the Phillips Academy, Andover, Massachusetts). Some bones were sent to the American Investigating Museum in Philadelphia "where they seem to have disappeared."

What is going on here? Were these humans or animals? An almost diabolical pattern of amazing evidence surfacing, then mysteriously vanishing, is evident all throughout history. We can imagine that some aspect of our society, perhaps religious or governmental, feels threatens by such finds and therefore suppresses them. But if that is not the case, a much more complex facet is revealed. Is there another dimension, filled with other creatures and agendas, of which they are in complete control? If you obtained a copy of the thunderbird photograph tomorrow, by the time you brought it to the newspaper, or your scanner, would it be a blank piece of paper? This kind of unsettling reality is most prevalent regarding those winged beings.

On September 12, 1880, the *New York Times* printed:

A marvelous apparition was seen near Coney Island. At the height of at least 1000 feet [305 m] in the air a strange object was in the act of flying toward the New Jersey coast. It was apparently a man with bat's wings and improved frog's legs. The face of the man could be distinctly seen and it wore a cruel and determined expression. The movements made by the object closely resembled those of a frog in the act of swimming with his hind legs and flying with his front legs....When we add that this monster waved his wings in answer to the whistle of a locomotive and was of a deep black color, the alarming nature of the apparition can be imagined. The object was seen by many reputable persons and they all agree that it was a man engaged in flying toward New Jersey.

Since March of 2000, a startling phenomenon has been widely witnessed, even videotaped multiple times, in Mexico and most recently Serbia. Flying humanoids have been seen soaring through the sky during broad daylight. They look eerily similar to superheroes flying around, sometimes even sporting a cape! According to *Rense.com*, in Mexico City, one of the videographers, Horatio Roquet, said of a sighting, "It looked like a human-shaped body 'standing' vertical and just floating over the roof. I was shocked. The figure was not facing me...I was looking straight at its right side. It was tall. No sound was heard and we both stood still, watching, while I continued recording."

Such reports are astounding, yet there is fairly clear video footage. So, what's happening here? Is this an elaborate hoax, witnessed by hundreds of people? Are they humans with a new technology? Aliens from another planet? Or do we finally have some evidence of these remarkable Mothman-like creatures? Or maybe they are batsquatch....

Bigfoot

Washington State has long been known for the hairy hominid called a sasquatch, but have you heard of the batsquatch? Reported for years near Mount Ranier and Mount St. Helens it's, sure enough, a flying bigfoot. Tell me that wouldn't raise the hair on your neck! While some say the batsquatch isn't, in fact, hairy, but has purplish, bald skin, appearing more like a pterodactyl, others say it looks just like a winged sasquatch.

On April 23, 1994, an 18-year-old named Brian Canfield drove his truck home alone, not far from Mount Ranier. You can imagine his shock when a tall "bigfoot-type creature" with bluish fur lowered from the night sky, landing in the middle of his headlight beams. The winged creature had a wolfish face, tufts on its ears, and shining, yellow eyes. Worst of all, Canfield's truck engine stopped mysteriously, leaving him to sit helplessly staring at the beast. The batsquatch gazed at the young man, both frozen for a bit, and then its powerful wings flapped, rocking the vehicle. The monster ascended and vanished into the night. Moments later, the truck engine came on, and Canfield hightailed it home in a frenzy.

"I believe his story," said C.R. Roberts, a reporter for the *Tacoma News Tribune* who interviewed the young man. "I believe he saw something that night...I have no idea what he saw." Such an opinion is perhaps surprising from a professional journalist. They are sizing up eyewitness testimony on a daily basis.

The most revealing aspect of the situation may reside in the location's history, though. That area is where pilot Kenneth Arnold saw UFOs next to his private plane June 24, 1947. In describing their appearance, he said "they flew erratic, like a saucer if you skip it across the water," coining the famous term, *flying saucer*. The following month, the infamous Roswell, New Mexico, crash occurred. Was the batsquatch an alien? Or is this just another example of how a warp-like location, attractive to UFOs, or at least allowing them to be seen, can also manifest phantimals?

Though we can't be certain of anything related to the batsquatch, one thing is for sure. Stories related to sasquatch prove them to be extremely elusive—so elusive, it may be difficult for some to believe they are physical, biological organisms. However, history shows a long line of confidence in similar creatures. The idea of a hairy, upright, man-like beast, such as the werewolf, was legally embraced in medieval times. In 1573, a hermit named Gilles Granier, was burned at the stake in France for being a supposed werewolf. But bigfoot, as the beast has been called since the late 1950s, has been embraced in modern times by many meticulous scientists who think he is simply a primatological cryptid. Those cryptozoologists are quick to say they don't "believe" in bigfoot—that "belief" is in the realm of religion. They simply "weigh evidence." Be as that may, we must consider the possibility that bigfoot is not a typical, biological organism. Even without wings, it is uncannily able to vanish, if sightings are authentic to begin with, that is.

I am certainly no cryptozoologist, and I don't pretend to have the body of knowledge available to those experienced researchers. As a person fascinated with mysteries, I do pay attention to the field, though. I own two casts of supposed footprints, and find the idea of this creature wondrous. I truly hope that bigfoot exists as an unknown primate and will one day be captured. In 2005, Loren Coleman was even involved in offering a $1-million bounty for evidence leading to capture of a live one. But I can't say with confidence I feel the evidence for sasquatch leans toward the creature being entirely a part of this realm. Though I don't greatly doubt he occupies this realm sometimes to a limited degree, it seems there should be even more evidence if he's here all the time. Maybe bigfoot is a phantimal, perhaps even the ghost of a prehistoric creature, similar to the enormous extinct possible ape, *Gigantopithacus*, or maybe even the spirit of a primitive human, though we have no solid record of such a giant stage in our direct past.

Bigfoot is often thought to be around 8 feet tall (2.4 m) and maybe 800 to 1000 pounds (363–454 kg). That's a big hunk of flesh and a massive amount of hair. The resources necessary to keep a population of such animals alive must be substantial. It simply seems there should be more hair on trees, more footprints, more dents in other surrounding animal populations if these creatures are thriving. I'm much more open to the possibility if they are only considered living deep in the middle of some twisted, uncharted wilderness, or hidden in the crags of bitter, snowy peaks. But there are bigfoot reports in virtually every single state in the United

States every year. Surely that is not realistic based on comparison to any other physical animal known. It might be more believable if sasquatch were the size of a mouse. Don't get me wrong, I'm not saying I don't think it's possible for them to exist as huge primates among us. I just think that, if they are, they certainly are seen much more rarely, under much more secluded circumstances, than most reports would have the average person believe. I don't think I find myself at odds with cryptozoologists in that point. But altogether, my gut instinct is that bigfoot, if real, has some special...power.

If bigfoot is a phantimal, that would help explain why he is seen so widely without leaving more physical traces. Otherwise, either people are highly misinterpreting other things they see (such as bears), are delusional, or are the victims of hoaxes. It could be a combination of all three. Though I haven't personally traveled far and wide searching for evidence of sasquatch, even I had a personal run-in with a hoaxer. The incident was obviously a waste of my time. But I value the experience because it's helpful in understanding how some people think. And, in retrospect, it was also somewhat humorous.

Years ago, I couldn't help but be excited when a stranger called and said "I've got a baby sasquatch!" Though I knew better than to believe, my mind was open. What if? What if, at long last, someone has captured one of these things and doesn't know who else to call but me? Surely obtaining a cute little baby would be easier than a big, badass adult, right? "How soon can you be here?" asked the man (I'll call him Clovis). I'd been up all night working and was weary, ready to hit the sack. Yet I told him I'd be right over. He was located in the mountains about 20 minutes from my house. Sure enough, there had been some bigfoot sightings in that area not too long beforehand.

When I arrived at his house, nothing looked out of place. He lived alone, except for two big German Shepherds, and the area was only slightly private. After very brief chit-chat I cut to the chase. "So where is he?" Clovis's head dropped and he sighed, taking a seat.

"My dogs ate him," he spoke sadly.

"Your dogs ate him?" I rolled my eyes.

"Yeah, the little fella was nearly dead when I found him. He was layin' outside when I went into the house to call some people."

"Why didn't you bring him inside?" I inquired.

"I was scared," his eyebrows rose. "I was afraid his momma might come for him and kill me." I nodded with a half-smile. "When I finally got outside, the dogs had nearly finished with him, but I still have some of the bones."

"You do?"

"Yeah, I've got his skull."

"Excellent," my mood brightened, "let's see it."

"Well..." a sense of hesitation overcame him, "I'm not sure I want to show it to you yet."

"And why's that?"

"Well I got to thinking,'" he said, "and this is just the first time I've met you. Maybe I should guard it a little more, think about this some. But I do have some other stuff I can show you?"

With that, a cardboard box emerged from below his table. Clovis settled down in full storytelling mode. He explained how he'd lived with sasquatch roaming around his home for years. And he'd been lucky to photograph them on quite a few occasions. He cracked open a large album, filled with dozens of 35mm prints. To my eye, each picture looked like a random shot of lush, green forest. "You see him there?" Clovis would ask with anticipation, pointing out a shot.

"No. Where?"

"Right there." Time after time, he'd point to some darkened area, probably a section of bark or twig, between leaves, declaring I should see a partially-hidden face staring back at me. "They're real good at hidin.'" I was becoming quite exasperated, about to head for the door. "But here's physical evidence," he noted.

This album was the sort with a large piece of clear plastic that would stick over each page, securing photos. But after the portion with images, he hailed a "gem." Sealed beneath the plastic was a long, slightly curled, coarse, black "hair."

"It's the best hair sample I ever got," he stated proudly, offering it for examination, so long as it was not removed. I took a loupe from my bag, and hunched over the artifact like a jeweler inspecting a diamond. At once, to my eye, the object's identity became obvious. It looked exactly like a black sewing thread. I could see millions of tiny wisps coming from it on all sides. Hairs, of course, have relatively smooth edges. That was the last straw for me, especially as he turned to serious talk of how he feared university scientists trying to take his evidence and "cut him" out of the picture.

As I was leaving, telling him I didn't feel he had anything in which I was interested, a look of desperation finally fell over his visage. "I...I tell you what," he said, "if you come back tomorrow, I'll show you the skull."

"Sorry," I replied, "but I don't have the time." With that, I left, and he seemed surprised that I hadn't bought his story. Though he didn't seem blatantly deranged, he was a blatant hoaxer. Upon arriving home, I called some fellow L.E.M.U.R. investigators to describe the weird experience. One of them was intrigued and wanted to go back the next day to see the skull. Clearly put out with the whole situation, I gave that investigator Clovis's number and said, "Call him yourself then." Sure enough, the next day the investigator went to view the sacred skull. Afterward, he called me with a report.

Clovis had indeed produced a small skull. However, the face was missing. He attributed this to the dogs, saying they had gnawed it away—a most unfortunate section to lose. Nonetheless, he still presumed the relic was a valuable chunk of evidence. He still would not allow the piece to be analyzed by experts, though. He "wasn't ready." Despite Clovis's story, the investigator said there were surprisingly clear saw marks, indicating the face had intentionally been removed. In fact, the portion cut away was nearly square! Though I'm not certain of the investigator's experience identifying remains, his feeling was that the bone was something like a turtle or squirrel skull.

Just because there are hoaxers, and something can be faked, that doesn't mean there are no genuine articles. Counterfeit $20 bills abound, but that doesn't mean there are no *real* $20 bills. I only relay this tale because it was a significant personal experience that shows how prominent hoaxing has become. Even though Clovis was not an intelligent manufacturer of false evidence, what if he had been? What if he'd spent years studying forensics and the expertise of sasquatch hunters? What if he'd been so good that I would have retold this experience differently? What if I'd used this fellow's props as evidence for the existence of a creature that may not exist as a normal, physical animal? Surely this has happened and does happen.

Unless we are to believe those who see bigfoot are imagining the experience, misinterpreting something else, or delusional, then we can say he is real. But is he a normal, biological organism? A good, determined scientist can make evidence for any creature seem plausible. Bigfoot is either completely physical, semi-physical, or doesn't exist at all. In my opinion, given our current selection of evidence, one should be open to all possibilities. At very least, maybe the physical creatures are prone to leaving apparitions behind, and many of the sightings are of those specters.

Water Monsters

Throughout history, perhaps the most prominent type of cryptids reported have been of the reptilian or amphibian class. In my mind, most notable of all are dragons. They are important because they've been recorded in virtually every major culture. Dragons are the only members of the Chinese astrological chart that are not known to exist factually, yet have been specified in Middle Eastern cultures (such as the Biblical reference to Leviathan in the book of Job), were feared in Greek mythology (such as the eight-headed Hydra slain by Hercules), and meticulously adorned European art. Vikings especially took pride in dragons, conquering for hundreds of years, a sinister dragonhead leading the way, lurching forward at the bow of deadly ships. Though the history and characteristics of these creatures are too vast for adequate summary here, such beasts have most always been associated with "supernatural" abilities. Whether it's the ability to breathe fire and lightning or magically heal with a glance, almost any wishful power can be projected onto them. Some could fly, some lived deep in the bowels of Earth, and others resided at the bottom of the sea, often guarding a treasure of profound importance.

It's possible the ancients' awareness of dragons relates to the age of dinosaurs. Though dinosaurs supposedly died long before humans were around, we can't know that for certain. In fact, we can't be entirely sure there aren't still a few around today (look at the coelacanth fish). This might explain early tales of enormous lizards. And some scholars speculate that primitive people, seeing the fireball of an inexplicable meteor blazing toward Earth, assumed it was a soaring, fire-breathing beast. That could be. Or perhaps dragons are phantimals of dinosaurs, aglow with plasma, materializing more easily during thunderstorms due to electrical activity. An observer might assume the ghost was actually creating the lightning. In fact, many cryptids look like dinosaurs, yet, just like the sasquatch, they cannot be proven as normal, physical entities, despite the efforts of many persistent researchers.

Current residents of the African Congo region speak of a water monster called mokele-mbembe. It means "one that stops the flow of rivers." Accounts of the monster were first recorded in 1776 by a French priest. Through the decades, numerous expeditions have been mounted to find the animal to no avail. At one point, natives were shown pictures of a sauropod dinosaur. They identified it as "mokele-mbembe." Sauropods were large, fat, four-legged herbivores with long necks and tails. Brachiosaurs were members of Sauropoda.

The most famous water monster, the Loch Ness creature, has long been described as a plesiosaur. Few realize just how enormous the loch is. It contains more fresh water than all of the other lakes in England and Wales combined, is nearly 1000 feet (305 m) deep, and has enough volume to store the entire human population of Earth multiple times. And if that weren't enough, its waters are so dark, due to peat, a diver's hand is usually not visible in front of his face. With those kinds of statistics, one could understand an actual, physical dinosaur remaining hidden. However, as is the case with so many cryptids, one would expect more of a peripheral impact, such as substantial dents in potential food sources.

Around the world, water monsters are often described as looking either serpent-like, or like plesiosaurs (with a large body, long neck, four flippers, and short, pointy tail). Technically, plesiosaurs were not dinosaurs, as they lived in the water and were related to lizards and turtles. Dinosaurs lived on land and were related to birds and crocodiles. Scientists believe plesiosaurs could have inhabited both fresh and salt water. Loren Coleman once pointed out to me that water monsters are sometimes seen crossing land, as well, indicating they might migrate. What are the chances some of these creatures are phantimals of animals long past?

The first question is how ghosts can manifest in water. If they are imprints, whether observed by internal, or external, means, then there is no need for a physical explanation of how their energy could materialize. On the other hand, if they are materializing in some objective form, like a plasma body, it would require an immense quantity of energy underwater, and is therefore unlikely. So, if water monsters are phantimals, they are probably imprints. There are accounts of ghostly objects over water all the time. I'm particularly fond of stories related to the Flying Dutchman, a spectral ship, glowing crimson, seen sailing around the Cape of Good Hope for nearly 200 years. It glides in, or just above, the ocean. Water, and especially salt water, is an excellent conductor of electricity, so perhaps that even enhances these mysterious effects.

In 2004, my team and I spent Halloween week cruising the Bermuda Triangle. We made a stop in the Bahamas to investigate pirate ghosts, but spent the rest of the time on the water. In 1492, Columbus witnessed weird illuminations over that area. And, sure enough, on Halloween night our expedition observed a white ball of light dancing in the distance. It followed our ship for an hour or more, keeping a steady pace. I asked experienced seamen if it was another vessel, but no one felt it was. Though it's difficult to conclusively identify such sights at sea under those conditions, we may have been seeing what Columbus described. And that may have indeed been of a phantasmal nature. Columbus wrote that his compass went haywire, and we observed two compasses onboard pointing in opposite directions. Though held far apart, they would never agree, and we could find no source of artificial magnetic contamination, of that magnitude, using our other equipment.

All that said, the most likely explanation for these water monsters is that they are indeed large, physical, biological organisms that are impossibly difficult to find in huge bodies of murky water. In 2005, Thai fisherman pulled a 646-pound (293-kg) catfish from the Mekong River. It was the size of a grizzly bear, an almost unbelievable sight, setting the world record for largest freshwater fish ever discovered. And guess what happened to the trophy? Is it carefully guarded behind a glass case in a prestigious museum, hundreds of awestruck tourists huddled around? Is it hanging above a rich oil tycoon's mantle? Is it being painstakingly dissected on a biologist's lab table? Nope. They ate it! This is a surprisingly common trend regarding cryptids. In 2005, the Laotian Rock

Rat (*Laonastes aenigmamus*) was discovered being sold at a meat market. Perhaps, in a remote gully of our planet, a group is devouring a delicious sasquatch thigh right now.

Imagine you're spending a peaceful day boating on the lake, the calm waters shining and breeze lightly rustling the trees. Maybe you even have a line in the water. And suddenly, the still is broken by the long, dark form of a slimy 646-pound (293-kg), 7-foot (2.1-m) long catfish back, surfacing just enough to see something *very tangible* is there. You would certainly describe that as a monster. There are also salamanders in the world that grow up to six feet (1.8 m) long, and, in the water, might appear quite a bit like a plesiosaur at a glance. Those kinds of creatures probably account for most of the water monster sightings. But couldn't they leave ghosts, as well?

The subject of cryptozoology is wonderful at its most basic level: There are indeed specimens of normal organisms, always existing in the present time and dimension, somewhere out there, hidden away on this great, huge planet. I feel to speculate on phantimals in no way demeans the hard-nosed fact-finding to which remarkable cryptozoologists devote their lives. I only suggest that life may exist on an even broader scale. Bodies of energy, nonphysical to us, are real. There is nothing in quantum physics that prevents an intersection between the animals of this dimension and those of others. After all, an atom is just an atom, and energy is just energy, here or there. We don't fully understand how combinations of atoms eventually lead to consciousness. Maybe everything is conscious in some way—there is no singular point at which "consciousness" simply springs to existence. Whatever the case, if a cryptid is purely physical, we should eventually find evidence. But if it is not, we will never find evidence that it is. At what point do we make the call? Answer: there is no point. All we can do is continue to push forward, forming hypotheses and theories with the best evidence we have. And, of course, those are the most enjoyable kinds of mysteries.

6 The Meaning of Pets in Life and Death

Dictionary.com defines *life* as "The property or quality that distinguishes living organisms from dead organisms and inanimate matter, manifested in functions such as metabolism, growth, reproduction, and response to stimuli or adaptation to the environment originating from within the organism." The smallest measurable unit of physical life is the *cell*. It is defined as "The smallest structural unit of an organism that is capable of independent functioning, consisting of one or more nuclei, cytoplasm, and various organelles, all surrounded by a semipermeable cell membrane." In a nutshell, a small, self-contained blob of matter, able to grow, reproduce, respond to stimuli and adapt to its environment is alive. Many organisms never make it beyond that stage.

I've always been fascinated by amoebas. I even wrote a children's book, in rhyming verse, called *The Lonely Ameba* ("ameba" is an alternate spelling of "amoeba"), tracking the adventure of Emo Ameba as he sets out to find a friend, encountering characters like Larry the Hairy Paramecium and Gena Euglena. Single-celled amoebas very much exemplify the most basic aspects of a living creature and nothing more.

They appear to be translucent, gelatinous blobs that can assume any shape. Amoebas have no brain, no eyes, no nose, no mouth, and no ears. And yet they clearly react to their environment. They avoid water with too much salt, as well as bright sunlight, yet seem to enjoy warm water, tending to stay in it and swimming more exuberantly. Upon encountering prey, they distort their pseudopods to wrap around and engulf it inescapably into their bodies. Once in a while, these asexual creatures split in half, reproducing by a process called binary fission. For all we know, to them, their lives seem as full and complex as ours do to us.

Amoebas and similar microorganisms are mysterious. What is it about these blobs that makes them alive? What is this invisible force filling them, driving them, making them aware? From where does it come? How is it contained in their thin, simple membranes? As primal as they are, with all our technology we cannot create one from scratch. Humans can't create anything from scratch. We always require pieces from Mother Nature, pieces that have been here long before humans, and then we use those building blocks to create something we call "new." Wouldn't it be something if amoebas were so much closer to the source of life that they understand more about the universe than we do? Yet they have no mouths to share that knowledge with others. Wouldn't that be almost fitting?

Scientists currently believe these single-celled creatures gradually evolved, over billions of years, into multi-celled animals. This chain reaction continued, and continues to this day. As the combinations of life branched into a complicated web of directions, the resultant organisms each became sensitive to those aspects of the environment useful for survival. Because of this, we have a wide and wonderful spectrum of animals that are able to gain information in unique ways.

Wonders of the Animal Kingdom

Penguins have a flat cornea. This enhances their vision underwater, allowing them to be superior hunters. Most extraordinary, they are also able to see ultraviolet (UV) light, invisible to human eyes. Bats can see into the UV range, as well. Ordinarily, a mammal's lens absorbs that frequency range, protecting the retinal cells. But nocturnal creatures never develop that protection because it's not a component of night-time survival. Many insects have an outstanding ability to see into the UV, especially bees. It not only helps them identify plants, widening the range of visible, distinct, patterns, but also assists in recognizing other insects whose wings often reflect UV light. Yet, oddly enough, bees cannot see the color red, easily visible to us, but too low a frequency for them.

On the other hand, some animals can detect the infrared (IR) range invisible to humans. Sources of heat produce IR waves, and humans literally glow with that energy. Perhaps the animals most sensitive to this are snakes in the pit viper family, such as rattlesnakes. Their name comes from two pits, or shallow holes, just behind the nostrils on either side of their heads that can detect thermal radiation, particularly beaming from warm-blooded prey. Scientists still are not sure how temperature changes stimulate the cells to activate neurons, but the process works with great efficiency. In fact, two pits seem to provide depth perception, just like two eyes. This allows a serpent to perceive its prey as a textured, three-dimensional form.

Considering the usefulness of two eyes, or eye-like organs, to give an observer depth perception, just imagine having eight eyes. Most spiders have four pairs of eyes, and this allows them to see a span of 360 degrees all at once. It's virtually impossible for us to imagine being able to see completely around ourselves all at the same time. Eyes can move up and down, left and right, in or out, for superior focusing. Such a trait is mind-boggling.

But regardless of an organism's ability to see a variety of light wavelengths and angles, the way light is processed by the brain makes a substantial impact. Humans appear to move in slow motion to insects like roaches or flies. This is because their brains are able to perceive, and make sense of, their surroundings much faster than ours. The effect is similar to the strobing phenomenon, but can be demonstrated more appropriately by the frame rate of a motion picture camera. Human action looks about normal when filmed 24 times per second, hence the traditional 24 frames per second (fps) as the rate for movies. If you shoot humans at a lower rate, like 18 fps, they appear to move in fast motion, like some of the old, black and white comedies of the early 20th century. If you shoot at 36 fps, the people move in slow motion. Some of the extreme high speed cameras, capable of filming thousands of fps, are used to slow down extremely fast subjects like speeding bullets.

This analogy between eye/brain coordination and cameras should help you understand why it's so darn hard to swat a fly. They see you coming like a lethargic, lumbering giant.

There are many creatures that can hear a broader range than humans. We can generally perceive from around 20-20,000 hertz. Basically, that means if air, ground, or some other medium is vibrating between 20 and 20,000 times per second, it resonates with our eardrums, creating a distinct sound. However, dogs can hear up to 40,000 hertz, cats up to 60,000, and small animals like rodents up to 100,000. The smaller your head, the higher you can hear because the size of your cranium usually determines the size of your resonant cavity. A big elephant hears very low, and can perceive 15 hertz or less. Because low waves travel farther than high ones, elephants use them to communicate over vast distances in the wild. Oddly enough, a pigeon can hear as low as 0.1 hertz!

Aside from how they can see and hear, animal abilities are different than human abilities in a rainbow of other ways. Pigs have often been criticized as unruly, uncouth eaters of slop. In fact, they have finer tastes than we do. Swine, and goats, have around 15,000 taste buds, whereas humans only possess about 9,000. Rabbits have 17,000, even better. These creatures with such expansive tastes are known for eating things we find disgusting. This must mean there are wonderful tastes in even soured and rotting items that we cannot appreciate. That's good for them, I suppose.

Of course taste and smell are generally interwoven in most species. We take advantage of earthworms on a daily basis, tossing them into water by the thousands as mere bait. And yet they, too, are remarkable. Their entire bodies are covered with aroma-detecting organs called chemoreceptors. Houseflies smell and taste by more than 3,000 receptors on their legs. Even feces is enjoyable to their advanced perception!

More mysterious are animals with a sixth sense for electromagnetism. Most notable are sharks. They seem to navigate by perceiving a three-dimensional map of their magnetic environment. And they can sense extremely tiny voltages, as low as 0.005 uV/cm. Some devices on the commercial market take advantage of this to protect scuba divers and surfers. Strong fields, overwhelming, disorienting, and disrupting to sharks are projected around the human. This makes the giant fish immediately turn and find more comfortable surroundings. Some have speculated a similar ability helps birds migrate, using the Earth's field as a map.

There is mixed data regarding how birds migrate so accurately over long distances, year after year. Many creatures, such as humans, have tiny traces of magnetite in their heads. These bits could act as compass needles, adjusting to the Earth's field. And, if the brain gains useful information from their position, this might assist in orienting an animal properly. However, according to Rupert Sheldrake's *Seven Experiments That Could Change the World*, this has been tested extensively with homing pigeons, but seems irrelevant. In 1969–70, William Keeton of Cornell University in Ithaca, New York, attached bar magnets to the heads and backs of pigeons, certainly enough to distort possible awareness of the Earth's subtle field. However, the birds were still able to home. Sheldrake notes:

> *Most of the published reports have failed to show any significant effects of magnetic fields,*

and in addition many other negative studies have remained unpublished. One of the leading investigators in the field, Charles Walcott, has come to the conclusion that: "Given the weight of all this negative evidence, coupled with the circumstantial nature of the positive evidence, it becomes very difficult to believe that the pigeon makes use of magnetic cues for its 'map.'"

Even more amazing is how some animals may respond not only to the Earth's terrain, but to bodies in space, as well. This is especially apparent in oysters, as described in *Supernature* by Lyall Watson. Marine biologist Frank Brown began experimenting with oysters in 1954 at his laboratory in Evanston, Illinois, near Chicago. It was well-known that oysters would open and close with the tide, spreading to ingest food at high tide, then sealing up at low tide. When Brown took groups of the creatures from Connecticut's shore to Evanston, a thousand miles away, the creatures retained their cycle of opening and closing, all in unison. But after two weeks, their timing changed.

The oysters began opening and closing at the time the tide would have reached Evanston, had it been on the coast. Perplexed by this, Brown surmised they might be adjusting by receiving cues from the variance in sunlight, so he locked them away in a completely dark, controlled chamber. This made no impact, as they still responded like clockwork. It seemed the oysters were actually sensitive to the lunar forces responsible for altering the tides: directly sensitive to a body over 250,000 miles (402,336 km) away! Watson claims the Hughes Aircraft Laboratory in California developed a "tilt meter" delicate enough to detect the moon's gravitational influence in a cup of tea. It makes one wonder how such lunar tides affect humans, being that we're primarily composed of water ourselves.

Though we can marvel at how receptive some animals are to energy fields, think of those creatures capable of *producing* extraordinary amounts. I have always been captivated by electric eels. Though they are not truly eels, but snake-like fish, these marvels of nature grow up to 9 feet (2.7 m) long, and produce up to 650 volts to stun or kill prey. Keep in mind, a standard electrical socket in the United States is only 110 volts. Their heads are negatively charged and tails positively charged, forming a long battery. The slimy cells capable of storing and conducting such current are still not completely understood by scientists. If we know biological components can generate this kind of power, it makes me wonder if some people possessing telekinetic ability, that is the psychic skill to affect matter without physically touching it, generate electromagnetic, or electrostatic, fields in a similar way.

Electrical forces associated with creatures remind us of the energy form that may reside after we die, as possibly evidenced by some Kirlian effects. This might be especially relevant for creatures that can regenerate missing limbs. A young salamander can grow a new leg in around a month. It takes longer for an adult, though, and the replacement is not as big and stout as the original. Though lacking a strong backbone, lizards commonly regenerate tails that have been bitten off by predators, and even possess a mechanism to help the tail snap off in a pinch. Frogs, crayfish, earthworms, and flatworms all have this ability to some extent. Some starfish can grow an entirely new creature from only a single arm. That means you could cut one starfish into five pieces to make five entirely new creatures! In college, my biology professor would speak of oyster fishermen annoyed by pulling starfish up in nets. Hoping to lower the population, since starfish eat oysters, the fishermen would cut them into pieces and dump the scraps overboard. Of course, the seamen inadvertently increased the starfish population at an amazing, exponentially expanding rate.

Biologists are intensely studying these regenerating organisms for a better understanding of how their bodies accomplish such a remarkable feat. Ideally, we could learn to adapt their genes for humans, allowing us to regrow limbs in the same way. In fact, a human child, up to the age of 11, can already regenerate an amputated fingertip. And on a regular basis, we regenerate to a smaller degree through normal healing and re-placement of internal parts like the linings of our stomachs and inside cheeks. The big question is whether or not, when animals such as starfish and lizards regenerate, the new cells are fitting into an energy mold that remains even after the physical sections are destroyed. Do their bodies provide an etheric blueprint, a ghostly form, by which the new limb's cells are guided?

This is just a small number of examples regarding what makes animals special. They have powers we do not possess. And if a human did have some of these abilities, we would certainly call that person "psychic." Because we all are made of the same substance—cells—the fact that some organisms have these char-acteristics proves that it is possible for biological entities to attain seemingly supernatural skills. It's another example of why we are egotistical, thinking that if we cannot personally perform something, it is an astounding accomplishment. Every organism is simply different in its own special way.

Brad Steiger is an expert on the psychic abilities of pets. He and his wife, Sherry, have even conducted extensive surveys regarding this issue and similar ones. I asked him his thoughts on how animals' extra senses might apply to a return from the dead. His reply:

> *Their returning from the dead is, in our opinion, evidence that our pets have souls. We all know the familiar story of the man who won't step into heaven once he finds that dogs are not allowed. Then, a few steps down the way, he discovers the true heaven, not the counterfeit, when dogs and pets are welcomed. Our surveys indicate that well over 80 percent of pet owners believe that their pet has a soul and that they will be reunited in their personal concept of heaven. Long before research into the paranormal and NDEs became popular, there were hundreds of accounts of men and women on their deathbeds being welcome by an image of a faithful old pet come to take them home. When the Lord speaks in the book of Genesis and gives humankind dominion over all animals, we translate "dominion" to mean "responsibility" to practice kindness and respect. When God breathes the breath of life into Adam, the verses later state that He/She did the same for animals. The breath that activates our bodies and ignites our spirits is the same one that grants those blessings to our animal companions.*

It seems a wide array of experiments could be done to specifically document the psychic abilities of animals. Imagine if a zoo were to team up with a group of statisticians and create tests for various types of psychic phenomena: precognition, telekinesis, clairvoyance, and so on. Would we find that one type of creature is more psychic than others? I suppose we would, at least in a certain area. Afterward, the DNA of that species could be analyzed for some possible clue as to why it possesses those skills. Might we then be able to adapt that DNA information for human usage? Here are Brad Steiger's thoughts about such a project:

> As long as these experiments are designed to bring absolutely no pain to the animal, I think the open-minded research into human/animal interaction, demonstrating our likes, rather than our differences, may be productive. It appears that there are numerous such tests being currently conducted. Science also constitutes of astute observation as well as laboratory experiments, and many scientists who own pets are excellent reporters of both physical and psychic interactions between humans and animals.

If I had to bet, I'd say reptiles might be the most psychic creatures. They seem to have the least ability to communicate through expressions. Look at how expressive most mammals are, for example. In order to compensate for that lack of expressive ability, it seems they may have evolved a stronger sense of mind-to-mind communication. Reptiles have ruggedly survived for so long that they must have some superior skills to judge their surroundings. And though their eyes are often cold and still, it might be the steady penetration of their gazes that can see so deeply into others, perhaps even drawing out the information needed. Though this is pure speculation, it emphasizes the need for proper testing. The more psychic an animal is, the closer it is to the afterlife. I imagine this acclamation to the beyond can help them return from the beyond, as well.

Worship of Animals

Perhaps the many special qualities of animals have somehow led to their worship throughout history. Even in biblical times, thousands of years ago, animals were considered sacred, hence sacrifices. In fact, Cain slew his brother Abel, considered the first murder by many, over this concept. When it came time to offer a sacrifice, Cain gave fruits and vegetables, but Abel offered "the firstlings of his flock and of the fat thereof." The Lord liked Abel's better and so, out of jealously, his brother killed him in the field.

Later on, during the Exodus story, the Jews decided to build a golden calf as an idol during Moses's absence. His brother, Aaron, was given the job:

> And Aaron said unto them, Break off the golden earrings, which are in the ears of your wives, of your sons, and of your daughters, and bring them unto me....And he received them at their hand, and fashioned it with a graving tool, after he had made it a molten calf: and they said, These be thy gods, O Israel, which brought thee up out of the land of Egypt. (Exodus 32:2–4)

When Moses returned and saw them worshipping the calf, he was so angry he smashed down the Ten Commandments, breaking the stone tablets. Afterward, he turned the idol into powder, spread it in water, and made the heathen worshippers drink their metal god. Did early people worship animals simply because they relied on them for sustenance, or did they apply deeper meaning to the creatures? After all, they could have chosen fruits or vegetables, just as Cain did. Why not make a huge, golden apple? A golden delicious, perhaps? (Sorry for the cheesy pun!)

Ancient Egyptians especially venerated Horus in falcons, and the ibis, a wading bird with a long curved bill. They also held bulls in divine regard. Around the region of Memphis, the bull Apis was considered the literal incarnation of a God. Scarabs, a type of dung beetle, represented Khepri. Scarabs would lay eggs in feces, and when they hatched, it appeared that life had mystically sprung from the lowest form of waste. This was fascinating to the Egyptians, and they perceived it as a form of rebirth. The God Khepri was considered custodian of the sun. Each day, he would renew its power, roll it into the sky (very much like a scarab rolling a ball of dung) and keep it safe for display the following day. Egyptians saw a parallel between Khepri's job and the life-giving power of scarabs.

During that same period, Greeks worshipped eagles as direct representatives of Zeus. Athena, the god of wisdom, manifested in owls. The god Dionysus ruled over wine, intoxication, civilization, law, and peace. He was symbolized by the bull, serpent, centaur, and satyr. However outlandish it may seem, creatures like satyrs are still seen today, a fringe of the cryptozoological compendium. They are half-man, half-goat beasts that roam the mountains. Oddly enough, recent reports of satyrs often note the entity speaks, an oddity for cryptids.

In 2005, *cryptomundo.com* posted a supposed satyr encounter from the 1990s. It occurred near Shreveport, Louisiana. A young woman claimed her brother had stepped outside for a cigarette when he heard a voice call his name. Immediately, he expected local children were hiding in the nearby vegetation, having a fun prank. And then "he caught sight of a 'hairy little man with horns' and retrieved a .22 caliber pistol from inside the house. He tried firing at the creature a couple of times, but it managed to evade him and laughed the whole time. It then leapt to the top of the fence, turned its head and smiled at him—revealing sharp teeth. The creature then bolted over the fence and apparently ran off into the woods."

These sardonic little entities, and similar ones, like centaurs (half-man, half-horse), are especially interesting. They indicate a belief that humans and animals are so closely related they can literally share the same physical body. This might help explain why animals are seen as not only sacred, but direct representatives of humane qualities. It should be noted that many scholars reject the notion that ancient Egyptians and Greeks actually worshipped animals. They feel it's an overstatement, implying a degree of barbarism on the part of those civilizations. Instead, they feel it's more accurate to say those cultures saw various animals as embodying the spiritual integrity of so many gods, and respected them as such—nothing more. This kind of philosophy might be more similar to the totem animals of Native Americans. Regardless of the interpretation, there's no doubting the bona fide worship of animals exercised by some cultures. Hindus are especially famous for this.

Hinduism is the third largest religion in the world, followed by around one billion people, mainly residents of India. It is based on the Vedas, a collection of sacred literature that dates back to at least 1500 BCE. The basic content of this text probably goes much farther back in the oral tradition, and some believe it has always existed since the beginning of time. In their faith, all living creatures have immortal souls and are reincarnated into various organisms. Because of this, many Hindus are strict vegetarians. Most sacred of all are cows, considered mother figures due to their production of milk. Killing or eating of them is prohibited in many sects. The full importance of cows is illustrated by holy verses in the Mahabharata:

> One should for three days drink the hot urine of the cow. For the next three days one should drink the hot milk of the cow. Having thus drunk for three days hot milk, one should next drink hot ghee (a type of butter) for three days. Having in this way drunk hot ghee for three days, one should subsist for the next three days on air only....

> One should never feel any repugnance for the urine and the dung of the cow. One should never eat the flesh of kine (cows). As the consequence of this, one is sure to attain to great prosperity.... One should always bathe, using cow dung at the time. One should sit on dried cow dung. One should

never cast one's urine and excreta and other secretions on cow dung.

Other animals, like monkeys, elephants, rats, and serpents, are also especially held in high regard. In the Rajasthan city Deshnoke, the Karni Mata Temple has grown quite famous. It's overrun by more than 20,000 rats, all revered. In the early 1900s, Maharaja Ganga Singh created the remarkable site as an ornate tribute to the goddess Karni Mata. Some Hindus believe Karni Mata cut a deal with Yama, the god of death: all the people of her tribe would be reborn as rats until they were finally reincarnated back to her clan as humans. Each year, thousands of people from around the world visit this temple, some as a mere curiosity, but most to worship the sprawling carpet of small, scurrying beasts.

Inside the shrine, one is not allowed to wear shoes. If a rat runs over a visitor's foot, it's a blessing of good luck. At any time, dozens of people can be seen kneeling like dogs, sipping from water and nibbling at food the rats have tasted—a divine privilege. The greatest thrill is catching a glimpse of a white rat. There are only a handful, and are said to be the goddess herself, along with close relatives. And if, God forbid, someone should accidentally stomp a rat to death, the least requirement is to replace it with a valuable rodent of silver or gold. Miraculously, there has never been a major outbreak of disease in this environment.

In nature, wild animals usually eat anything they are capable of capturing and digesting. That's a basic component of evolution and survival of the fittest. Why have humans treated animals any differently? If Hindu cultures have venerated cows for thousands of years, why have other cultures gobbled them up without hesitation? Worshipping animals, as opposed to eating them, seems to defy the natural urge to consume whatever nutrition is available. Surely this exemplifies a state of mind that transcends primal instinct, paying homage to the special qualities animals possess. On a much lesser scale, is this why we value their companionship so much as pets?

I am not a pet enthusiast to an extreme degree. Frankly, I don't even like the idea of having a dog or cat in my bed, though I've often accepted the situation due to my girl-friend's wishes. Allowing a canine to lick my face is out of the question, and though the death of a pet is sad, it cannot, and should not, be equated with that of a human in any way. Those are my personal opinions, and I'm sure many reading this book will gravely disagree. Though I am not fanatically enthusiastic about such companions, I still find them utterly fascinating. Many people may find animals captivating by imagining the creatures somehow share a similar mindset to humans—they project human characteristics onto the pet. Though we all demonstrate similar emotions to some extent, I find them compelling for the opposite reason: We are so different.

The very fact animals perceive the world so diversely gives us an exciting opportunity. They are like cameras that can capture an experience beyond our current technology. There is no machine nearly as intricate and complex as those of flesh and blood that are slowly, painstakingly crafted by nature. Their superhuman abilities alone, whether seeing, hearing, tasting, smelling, or feeling more, might escalate some connection between them and us. Maybe we enjoy pets so much because they can sense something deeper, more meaningful, about us, than even other humans. People are extremely distracted creatures. Our civilization, our systems of government and prosperity, demand we focus each day on achieving particular goals to earn money and fulfill societal expectations. But our pets are not as distracted by that lifestyle. They have more time to absorb reality for what it is in the true, present sense. Does that allow them to be more receptive to who we really are, or at least aspects of ourselves blatantly beyond our own comprehensions? Like the microscopic amoeba, are they somehow closer to the ultimate meaning of life and creation, a truth so basic and fundamental that we've strayed far away in our manufactured system?

Most people become magnetically attached to their pets over time. The simple desire to care for something weaker and seemingly less intelligent may explain a lot. But is there an aspect of the relationship on an almost metaphysical level? History seems to answer with a resounding yes. And each day, science proves more and more why that connection may exist—they can experience a world more vast than the one we experience in a multiplicity of ways. The impending death of a pet is all the more complex because of this.

Generally, as a society, we have a clear appreciation for human life. If something can be done to save a person, we do it, no matter the cost. There is no level of financial depth too deep, or emotional hardship too intense, if it results in saved lives. Commonly, people give their lives, and the lives of their loved ones (as in war), to ultimately save others. But when it comes to animals, the scale shifts to a degree that causes much frustration and pain.

When you go to the vet with your beloved, ailing dog, and are given a melancholy choice, you are torn. "We can do an operation for $2,500 and he might live," says the doctor. "Or he might not; it's a 50/50 situation," what choice do you make? If you are wealthy, and won't miss $2,500, then the choice is much easier. You can spend the money and take the gamble. But most people cannot take a chance, throwing that kind of money down the drain. After all, no matter how much money you have, nothing and no one lives forever. Is it worth it? *That* is the painful question. Like it or not, you are required to place a definite value on life. If it were the same amount to save a parent, spouse, or child, there would be no debate. Financial hardship would be endured and the money found. But it's at that point when we must place the value of our pets in true perspective. Most of us will have the pet "put down" and feel terrible afterward.

When your pet is cold and dead, what becomes of that special connection? How is that absence, even an inevitable sense of guilt, reconciled? After all, as caretakers of our pets, we must feel guilty upon their deaths, however illogical. It's only natural to think *somehow* you could have done *something* differently. But again, to be realistic, you have to understand that everything must eventually die and that matter is beyond your control. That situation can be dealt with in a number of ways, and mourning is never simple nor easy. But what are the chances your pet will come back? In life, they already can sense, and are connected to, other realities. Does that give them an upper hand, allowing them to return more easily, even more than a human perhaps? Why not?

No one can be certain of what a dying person experiences. Even those who've had near-death experiences (NDEs) often report perceptions unique to themselves. And besides, near death is not the same as death, because NDE victims come back. But we all know about the light at the end of the tunnel. "The light," is such a well-known aspect of the death experience that speaking of it has become a cliché. "Go to the light!" or "Don't go to the light!" If there is some measure of accuracy in describing one's relationship to the light, it suggests one should sometimes know, and make a conscious effort, to go into it, advancing to another stage of existence. Does an animal understand this? Perhaps some animals naturally go for the peaceful illumination, yet others may fear it. Maybe the experience of death is even more confusing for an animal who cannot rationalize the situation like a human. That, and a dependence on human masters, may also increase the chances of a pet ghost sticking around. They rely on us for guidance in life, and why should that change in the instant of death?

Many of us do not worship animals enough to drink their urine and bathe in their feces. Most of us can fully appreciate our pets while feasting on a juicy hamburger, as well (perhaps even sharing). And yet we do revere them. They are special, and capable of sensing things about us, and the world, beyond our own perception. That same ability may assist them in returning from the other side, or even slipping back and forth. We are not so different from them—all of us the end result of a single cell that apparently emerged from the void as perhaps nothing more than a concentrated bit of thought and intention. It's wrong to consider ourselves superior to them just because we've taken them into our homes.

That egocentric human view makes us think we truly rule the world. Yes, we have the nuclear bombs and could blow it all to specks in a moment. We might die, but not all life. Microorganisms and insects would still abound. The old urban legend is true: cockroaches really could survive a nuclear explosion better than humans. Look at the enormous size of beasts in the past, like dinosaurs, and yet they died off, the Earth inherited by smaller, more efficient organisms, like us. Why should the trend not continue, with our dominion eventually surrendering to even smaller and more-efficient, durable life-forms? Hasn't it already? Couldn't an invisible microbe kill us all off tomorrow? Either way, whether we die from a nuclear holocaust or the catastrophic crash of an immense meteor, how many of those microscopic critters would miss us? How many even know we exist this very second? To them, I presume we are not fellow animals, but an *environment*, and our bodies must seem as huge and mysterious as the infinite cosmos is to us. And for that matter, all of us on Earth may simply be parasites living in the cells of some behemoth creature beyond our comprehension, the planets orbiting like subatomic particles. Perhaps, as some Native Americans believed, the world rests safely on the back of a giant turtle.

Sometimes I look at my dog or cat and think carefully about our relationship. I do all the work, pay all the bills, provide all the food and water, healthcare, and protection. And I wonder, who's really in control here? Am I? Or am I just the slave of this pet, the one who does all the work while it lounges around relaxing all day long. Does that really make me the superior one? Or is it just the opposite? Maybe those glassy little eyes, dosing and half-open, conceal a mind that has it all figured out, and has for thousands of years—a life of luxury at my expense. Are *we* the pets, serving our masters? Maybe they're even smarter than we think they are.

Conclusion

The ghost of Nellie, my miniature daschund, was only around about a week. Although I'm a paranormal investigator, I probably wouldn't have known she was around if it weren't for her shrill whimpering in the night. I often say though I enjoy researching haunted houses, I don't want to live in one. Because of that, I rarely investigate my own home. On a few occasions, I suspect paranormal entities may have followed me from someplace else, and in those cases, the gear has been employed, but that's a rarity. With Nellie, though, the presence was undeniable.

I took lots of photos, but none of them showed her. I attempted to record her sounds, yet none of my audio devices could capture them. Was it all an illusion? Was I only imagining she were there? I, like most people, would probably have believed that and thought nothing more. But, of course, I have tools that most do not: electromagnetic and electrostatic detectors. I would place them on the floor at areas where Nellie liked to spend time, then I'd kick back, relax, and observe for hours. Eerily, eventually I could hear the sounds, faint at first, then growing.

Though the space before me looked vacant, just a tile floor in the kitchen for example, beside empty food and water bowls, *something* was there. As my ears perceived her sounds, a small field of energy moved around the kitchen, low to the floor, though everything else was still. It reminded me of the manx cat ghosts at Cynthia's house. The fields were exactly as prominent as I'd expect from her living physical form, and yet it was not there. As days passed, the strength of her field gradually lessened until, finally, it was gone. What could this mean?

I didn't speak to the presumed spirit, other than calling it toward my meters. And my ability to measure the anomalies was inconsistent, a perpetually frustrating aspect of conducting this sort of research. I can imagine that, as time progressed, something about her specter dwindled. In fact, in this particular instance, I think her ghost was a noninteractive imprint. And though aspects of this imprint were prominent enough to create notable field disturbances, some part of the manifestation could only be perceived by my naked, subjective hearing. The ability of my ears to be sensitive, when my microphones were not, helps reinforce the concept of antenna-receiver relationships.

Quite simply, any antenna that receives a frequency is also capable of broadcasting that frequency, and vice versa. If you reverse the connections, a speaker can become a microphone and a microphone a speaker. On an even more mechanical level, if you apply a sufficient battery to a motor's terminals, the motor will spin. But if you spin a motor, the motor's terminals will generate electricity. By the same token, whatever special energy biological organisms broadcast—maybe that of *mind*—can be detected by other biological organisms; and perhaps *only* other biological organisms because our manufactured technologies, however advanced, are not as superbly developed as life-forms. Could this be why I could hear the daschund's calls? That possibility, and its overall implications, seem logical to me.

Our ability to understand phantimals may depend on our ability to understand quantum physics. Though the idea of comprehending parts of quantum physics may seem daunting, it's really not, unless you want to grasp the mathematical equations or let the philosophical ramifications sink in.

In December of 2005, the *New York Times* printed an article called "Quantum Trickery: Testing Einstein's Strangest Theory." Physicists at the National Institute of Standards and Technology in Boulder, Colorado, have been able to make atoms spin in two different directions at the same time:

> *These* [half dozen beryllium] *atoms were each spinning clockwise and counterclockwise at the same time. Moreover, like miniature Rockettes they were all doing whatever it was they were doing together, in perfect synchrony. Should one of them realize, like the cartoon character who runs off a cliff and doesn't fall until he looks down, that it is in a metaphysically untenable situation and decide to spin only one way, the rest would instantly fall in line, whether they were across a test tube or across the galaxy.*

Physicists call this a "cat state":

> *No, they were not sprawled along a sunny windowsill. To a physicist, a "cat state" is the condition of being two diametrically opposed conditions at once, like black and white, up and down, or dead and alive.*

Did you catch the part about "dead and alive?" If necessary, let me clarify what this means. Scientists have measured the same object moving in two different directions at the same time. Don't even try to comprehend that one—it's so foreign to our usual way of thinking that it's virtually impossible to truly grasp. For now, just keep it in mind. Secondly, that particle is connected to other particles even though there is no direct relationship. In other words, two different points at opposite ends of the universe are somehow connected, like opposite ends of a wormhole. This demonstrates that space and time are completely flexible. Let me put it this way: we've proven that anything is possible.

If we've proven that an object can simultaneously move in two completely opposite directions at once, think about the spectrum of possibilities in between those extremes. Such a mind-boggling reality can explain anything, regardless of how bizarre. On the other hand, saying anything is possible is the same as saying nothing is possible. That's where things can get confusing. So let's cut through it as distinctly as possible.

Our society is used to thinking about things in a very simplistic, linear way. We're not so different from animals in that sense. We think within the three dimensions: up and down, left and right, back and forth. But, in fact, the universe has other dimensions for which we don't have obvious sensory organs (like eyes and ears). But, as time proceeds, we will hopefully develop our senses more as we accept and believe that there is more information available. After all, if all life descended from an original cell, compare ourselves to amoebas. It took a long time for the eyes, ears, noses, and mouths to congeal so prominently. To try to understand my experience with Nellie in terms of pure energy broadcast linearly, like an AM radio show, may be a relevant but far oversimplified way of viewing the situation. That is why my equipment was limited to a degree beyond my brain. After all, when I say my naked ears could hear her, what I really mean is that my brain could hear the sounds. The ears just funnel along the vibrations for the brain to interpret.

Quantum physics continues to emphasize that no point in the universe is separate from any other point. No time is lost in oblivion, separate from any other point in time. And if opposite conditions can occur at once, you can definitely be alive and dead at the same time. This is the cutting edge of our knowledge, and that's why it's natural to not truly understand what it all means. But what else can you expect? Trying to explain how a television or microwave works to Socrates might not be that easy—and he lived less than 2,400 years ago, an extremely short period given our discussions of, and evidence for, dinosaurs that lived 65 million years ago.

As time progresses, we learn, in greater detail, that magic is real. I don't use the term "magic" to describe a certain practice, but to say that any phenomenon is capable of manifesting in reality. Our physical laws are only based on the most likely outcomes, the probabilities, within the frequency range that garners most of our attention. The possible and probable are two entirely different things. It is improbable that most people will see a ghost. But it is exceedingly possible as human awareness increases more with time. You may think human cognizance of spiritual matters was more prevalent in ancient times due to superstition. But was it really? Wasn't the world a far more violent place thousands of years ago than it is now? You might say that's because we now have wonderful technology to help prevent crimes, but why is there the will to use those tools for that purpose? I'd like to think it's due to a greater spiritual awareness as civilization proceeds. As we grow in intelligence, hopefully we realize the impact of our behaviors and need for spiritual enlightenment more than our caveman ancestors did.

Imagine living in ancient times without nature programs on television, without a full set of encyclopedias, without libraries, the Internet, without even widespread literacy. Imagine a time when the world was not necessarily flat or round, but an immense slab of dirt, barren or lush, sometimes rising in majestic ridges and peaks, sometimes falling to treacherous canyons, always leading to crashing ocean waves, alongside an infinite, blue sky. And why, at night, did the glowing, orange ball turn into a white one, and so many crumbs of light appear in the black sky, like a million tiny eyes or shining windows into some other world? Try to imagine the beasts we know to be real today as wild anomalies, fodder for half-true tales, authentic monsters. Now our zoos are spread far and wide, accessible to all, kindergarteners and adults, for a nominal fee. And yet, even in this age, animals still surprise us, amaze us with their perceptions of information and realms invisible to our senses, make us speculate on exactly what they can do and how they do it. How can we be surprised when they seem to push the envelope further, appearing as part of some other realms as opposed to simply perceiving them?

To read ancient documents and see animals portrayed in mysterious ways, part physical and part not, can be seen as either evidence of ancient ignorance or the documentation of an outstanding event. Either way, it displays the amount of reverence, good or bad, for the idea of animals in relation to people.

In the Bible's Book of Daniel, the arrogant king Nebuchadnezzar is punished by being transformed into an animal-like beast of the field for seven years:

> *While the word [was] in the king's mouth, there fell a voice from heaven, [saying], O king Nebuchadnezzar, to thee it is spoken; The kingdom is departed from thee.*
>
> *And they shall drive thee from men, and thy dwelling [shall be] with the beasts of the field: they shall make thee to eat grass as oxen, and seven times shall pass over thee, until thou know that the most High ruleth in the kingdom of men, and giveth it to whomsoever he will.*
>
> *The same hour was the thing fulfilled upon Nebuchadnezzar: and he was driven from men, and did eat grass as oxen, and his body was wet with the dew of heaven, till his hairs were grown like eagles' [feathers], and his nails like birds' [claws]. (Daniel 4:31-33)*

This is an example of how ancient people equated animal qualities with being not only disgusting, but even anti-God, if not downright demonic. Of course, no one wants to transform into another animal, such as a werewolf, but it does prove that thousands of years ago animals were seen as less divine. I am quite content being a human, as opposed to whatever beast the king became, and yet I can't say that animals are less divine than us. How can we believe that when we are all made of the same substances?

Animals have, therefore, fit many molds, as needed, throughout history. As seen by the dual role of the snake in Exodus, or the dove-like spirit that landed on Jesus upon his baptism, their sense of mystery is what makes them pliable for our symbolism. They can be horrors, saints, or something in-between, related to man in bizarre fashions. On top of that, if we consider their abilities to transcend the physical altogether, they certainly represent the most remarkable qualities of possible life.

If we, like our animal colleagues, are simply more complex variations of single-celled blobs of life, then perhaps we're all slipping back and forth, from this frequency range to others, on cycles both small and massive, lifetimes apart. And some of the creatures we know about are engulfed in the world at a different frequency of perception. To examine the mysterious qualities of those animals catalogued in museums and zoos and then make the leap to cryptids, such as Mothman or bigfoot, is not so drastic. Because science and exploration allow us to solve the easiest enigmas first, where does that leave us now? In this day and age of startling, compact-computer technology in daily lives, and the incredible results of quantum physics experiments in the lab, what realms of life might we soon find for the first time?

Enjoy your pets, and all living things in your environment, for their warmth, beauty, and complexity. But also see them as subjects in your personal laboratory—this great, vast environment of growing, expanding, oscillating life—so we can learn even more. Just as you can never dip into the same river twice, every part of everything around you is in a constant state of change. This is most dramatically evident with dynamic, living cells. They embody the ultimate mystery: Where did we come from and where are we going? By employing some of the basic knowledge and techniques in this book, you can start the process of scientific inquiry on your own.

Each year, I do plenty of speaking engagements. From time to time, someone asks me the hardcore, ultimate question: What is the meaning of life? It's generally followed by a rolling chuckle from the crowd. However, I have an answer. Many think of God as some omniscient, omnipotent being who sits at peace, swaying reality according to judgment far greater than we could ever attain. If so, I feel sorry for God. Think of how boring that would be—to know everything, to have control over everything. In the long run, it would amount to no excitement. Mystery is what drives life. I believe the meaning of life boils down to one word, plain and simple: *motion.* Every part of our universe can either sit still or move. Sometimes the motion will be constructive, other times destructive. These concepts, along with ideas of good and evil, are subjective. Are you evil if you kill and eat a person? Probably. But is a bear? Probably not. See what I mean by subjective?

Even when living things appear to be still, they're vibrating at a minuscule level more than those things we consider inanimate. Whether it's you, your dog, a giraffe, or a paramecium, we living creatures possess a form of energy that is dynamic. We may not have it forever, as it slips from cell to cell, being to being, as some parts die and others gain it, and that's why it's important to grasp it while it's here for you. Looking at ourselves is difficult, because the view is largely in one direction. And so we should look to our closest relatives—humans, humanoids, and animals—but especially our pets.

We are a part of the animals around us, indistinguishable from them at the smallest level. By looking at them, appreciating their special senses, and learning from their transitions between this realm and others, we can understand more about ourselves. When we compare their superpowers to ours, and ours to theirs, a balance is struck, an essential equilibrium designed by millions of years. This, more than anything, reveals the true wonder of nature and full spectrum of life. Between us, we can fly, breathe underwater, hibernate, regenerate amputated limbs, change colors, withstand the vacuum of space, see into frequencies high and low, have the strength of Hercules, and move at sensational speeds. Whatever God is, we can know God through creations. Each day we learn more, and some of those creations we have only glimpsed thus far. Keep your mind and eyes wide open. If you blink, you may miss the next one.

In this book, we've pondered the definition of a pet, and how we separate pets from animals in general. Perhaps, first and foremost, the reason we call them "pets" is because we pet them. Each time you share a moment of affection with your animal, think about what must be running through your animal's head. That is probably the key to the strongest bond obtainable, even capable of bringing them back from the other side—trying to understand them, hoping they understand us. We should both learn from each other. I'd like to think we're all on the same boat, simply trying to make it through life the best way possible, using whatever gifts nature has given. At that level, if on no other, we are surely the same.

Glossary

androgynous Not clearly male or female.

apparition A supernatural image of a person, animal, or thing; often used as a synonym for ghost.

beacon A bright light that is used to help people find their way.

elemental A being that, though generally not of our physical world, sometimes appears in it.

entity A self-aware, interactive being that has its own independent existence.

harbinger An animal that exhibits or is aware of spiritual energy.

hybrid Something that is a combination of two different things.

imprint A being that is neither self-aware nor interactive, but may be a glimpse into the past.

Inquisition An organization in the Catholic Church that sought out and published those who did not accept its authority.

luminous Giving off, or seeming to give off light; glowing.

manifest To become visible; to reveal oneself.

minion One who follows the orders of a powerful leader or master.

Occam's Razor The rule, in science or philosophy, that the simplest solution to a question is the most likely one.

oscillation Moving back and forth with a regular rhythm.

paranormal Having to do with events or phenomena that have no known scientific explanation.

phantimal A paranormal creature that appears more animal-like than human-like.

precursor A person or thing that comes before another person or thing.

rationalize To try to come up with a logical explanation for something.

realm An area or sphere in which something lives, takes place, or exists.

séance A gathering at which people try to contact the dead.

subjective Reflecting a person's opinions, feelings, or personal viewpoint.

synchronistic Happening at the same time, especially in a way that cannot be rationally explained.

transient Not permanent; lasting or staying somewhere only for a short period of time.

zoologist A scientist who studies animals and their behavior.

For More Information

Animal Planet
One Discovery Place
Silver Spring, MD 20910
(240) 662-2000
Website: http://www.animalplanet.com
This television network is part of Discovery Communications.
It has aired a wide range of shows about animals,
including *Finding Bigfoot* and *The Haunted*, a show about
animal ghosts.

Bigfoot Discovery Museum
5497 State Route 9
Felton, CA 95018
(831) 335-4478
Website: http://bigfootdiscoveryproject.com
Affiliated with the Bigfoot Discovery Project, this museum
had its grand opening in 2006. Visitors to the museum can
watch the famous Patterson/Gimlin film, made in 1976.
The museum's curator and co-founder, Michael Rugg, is a
longtime Bigfoot enthusiast.

International Cryptozoology Museum
11 Avon Street
Portland, ME 04101
Website: http://cryptozoologymuseum.com
As you might imagine, this museum is dedicated to the
study of cryptids. The museum opened in its current

location in downtown Portland in 2009. The basis of its collection was founder Loren Coleman's own cabinet of curiosities.

The Metropolitan Museum of Art
1000 5th Avenue
New York, NY 10028
(212) 535-7710
Website: http://www.metmuseum.org
Home to an extensive collection of ancient Egyptian art, the Met, as it is often known, is a great place to visit to get a sense of the importance of animals in ancient Egyptian culture. Among the artifacts on display are cat mummies and an array of animal statues.

The Mothman Museum
411 Main Street
Point Pleasant, WV 25550
(304) 812-5211
Website: http://www.mothmanmuseum.com
Visitors to this museum can learn more about the Mothman sightings that transfixed the Point Pleasant area during the 1960s. The museum has a visual media room that shows documentaries on the phenomenon, as well as a collection of memorabilia and props from the 2002 movie made about it.

The Natural History Museum
Cromwell Road
London SW7 5BD
England
+44 (0)20 7942 5000
Website: http://www.nhm.ac.uk

One of the many treasures that this major English museum houses is a skull that has been identified as the Beast of Bodmin Moor, a cat-like apparition that is believed to appear on Bodmin Moor, in Cornwall, England.

Penn State Paranormal Research Society
121 Thomas Building
State College, PA 16802
Website: https://sites.google.com/site/pennstateprs/home
This organization, affiliated with Penn State University, hopes to educate the public about paranormal research. It offers presentations about the paranormal and carries out investigations of paranormal phenomena.

Windsor Great Park
The Crown Estate Office
The Great Park
Windsor SL4 2HT
England
+44 01753 860222
Website: http://www.thecrownestate.co.uk/windsor/windsor -great-park/
Windsor Forest is the hunting grounds of the fearsome Herne the Hunter, a ghostly figure wearing deer horns who appears astride an equally ghostly black steed. Today, what remains of the forest is part of Windsor Great Park.

Websites

Because of the changing nature of Internet links, Rosen Publishing has developed an online list of websites related to the subject of this book. This site is updated regularly. Please use this link to access this list:

http://www.rosenlinks.com/TTOT/Cat

For Further Reading

Bartholomew, Robert E. *The Untold Story of Champ: A Social History of America's Loch Ness Monster.* Albany, NY: State University of New York Press, 2012.

Belanger, Melissa. *The Ghost Hunter's Survival Guide: Protection Techniques for Encounters with the Paranormal.* Woodbury, MN: Llewellyn Publications, 2009.

Blackburn, Lyle. *Lizard Man: The True Story of the Bishopville Monster.* San Antonio, TX: Anomalist Books, 2013.

Burnette, Tom, and Rob Riggs. *Bigfoot: Exploring the Myth & Discovering the Truth.* Woodbury, MN: Llewellyn Publications, 2014.

Crain, Mary Beth. *Haunted Pet Stories: Tales of Ghostly Cats, Spooky Dogs, and Demonic Bunnies.* Guilford, CT: Globe Pequot Press, 2011.

Doyle, Arthur Conan. *The Hound of the Baskervilles.* New York, NY: Oxford University Press, 2009.

Ellis, Melissa Martin. *The Everything Ghost Hunting Book: Tips, Tools, and Techniques for Exploring the Supernatural World.* 2nd edition. Blue Ash, OH: Adams Media, 2014.

Gerhard, Ken. *Encounters with Flying Humanoids: Mothman, Manbirds, Gargoyles & Other Winged Beasts.* Woodbury, MN: Llewellyn Publications, 2013.

Godfrey, Linda S. *American Monsters: A History of Monster Lore, Legends, and Sightings in America.* New York, NY: Tarcher, 2014.

Irving, Washington. *The Legend of Sleepy Hollow and Other Stories from the Sketch Book.* New York, NY: Signet Classics, 2006.

Newman, Rich. *Ghost Hunting for Beginners: Everything You Need to Know to Get Started.* Woodbury, MN: Llewellyn Publications, 2011.

Newton, Michael. *Hidden Animals: A Field Guide to Batsquatch, Chupacabra, and Other Elusive Creatures.* Santa Barbara, CA: Greenwood, 2009.

O'Donnell, Elliott. *Animal Ghosts: Animal Hauntings and the Hereafter.* Revised and Updated by John E. L. Tenney. lulu.com, 2012.

Rainbolt, Dusty. *Ghost Cats: Human Encounters with Feline Spirits.* Springfield, TN: Lyons Press, 2007.

Redfern, Nick. *Monster Files: A Look Inside Government Secrets and Classified Documents on Bizarre Creatures and Extraordinary Animals.* Pompton Plains, NJ: New Page Books, 2013.

Sheridan, Kim. *Animals and the Afterlife: True Stories of Our Best Friends' Journey Beyond Death.* Carlsbad, CA: Hay House, 2006.

Smith, Penelope. *Animals in Spirit: Our Faithful Companions' Transition to the Afterlife.* New York, NY: Atria Books, 2008.

Warren, Joshua P. *How to Hunt Ghosts: A Practical Guide.* New York, NY: Touchstone Books, 2003.

Warren, Joshua. *It Was a Dark and Creepy Night: Real-Life Encounters with the Strange, Mysterious, and Downright Terrifying.* Pompton Plains, NJ: New Page Books, 2014.

Zullo, Allan. *Haunted Pets: True Ghost Stories.* New York, NY: Scholastic, 2013.

INDEX

About the Author

Joshua P. Warren was born in Asheville, North Carolina, and has lived in the Blue Ridge Mountains his entire life. At the age of 13, he wrote his first published book. Since then, he has had nine books published, including the regional best-seller, *Haunted Asheville*, and *How to Hunt Ghosts*, and is the president of his multimedia productions company, Shadowbox Enterprises, LLC. His articles have been published internationally, and he has been covered by such mainstream periodicals as *Southern Living, Delta Sky, FATE, New Woman, The New York Times, FHM*, and *Something About the Author*; and even made the cover of the science journal, *Electric Space Craft*, published by NASA Hall-of-Fame engineer Charles Yost. A winner of the University of North Carolina Thomas Wolfe Award for Fiction, he wrote columns for the *Asheville Citizen-Times* from 1992 to 1995. His first novel, *The Evil in Asheville*, was released in 2000.

An internationally-recognized expert on paranormal research, Warren was hired by the famous Grove Park Inn Resort to be the **Photo courtesy of JoshuaPWarren.com.**

first person to officially investigate the Pink Lady apparition in 1995 (the same year he founded L.E.M.U.R. paranormal investigations, of which he is president). Warren also led the expedition that captured the first known footage of the elusive Brown Mountain Lights, eventually resulting in scientific breakthroughs, via experiments Warren led in the lab, that help explain most of the lights and many mysterious, natural plasmas (such as ball lightning) that occur around the world. His work has been praised by the Rhine Research Center, The North Carolina Center for the Advancement of Teaching (or NCCAT, for which he gives annual presentations) and numerous scholars such as *New York Times* best-selling author Dr. William R. Forstchen, Dr. William Roll, Dr. Andrew Nichols, and Oak Ridge National Laboratory engineer David Hackett.

Photos courtesy of JoshuaPWarren.com.

Warren has appeared on the Discovery Channel, Travel Channel, History Channel, and numerous networks and/ or affiliates of NPR, CNN, ABC, NBC, and CBS. He is frequently asked to be a guest on radio shows around the world, especially *Coast to Coast AM* with George Noory/ Art Bell. Warren is also an international award-winning filmmaker (including Hollywood.com's Top Underground

Filmmaker of 1998), having worked on many sets, such as Warner Brother's *My Fellow Americans*, Universal's *Patch Adams, Paradise Falls, Inbred Rednecks, Songcatcher, Sinkhole*, and *The Devil of Blue Mountain.*

Warren works as a radio host for Clear Channel, the largest radio corporation in the world, and currently has an exclusive television contract with Discovery. For more information, see www.JoshuaPWarren.com.